A BOOK OF ESSAYS

EDITED BY ROBERT CHAMBERS

A Book of Essays

AND CARLYLE KING

MACMILLAN OF CANADA · TORONTO

ST. MARTIN'S PRESS · NEW YORK

ISBN 0-7705-0341-1

Library of Congress Catalog Card No. 64-14130

Printed in Canada
Reprinted 1964, 1966, 1970, 1971, 1972

ACKNOWLEDGMENTS AND COPYRIGHT NOTICES

'The Flag of the World' from *Orthodoxy* by G. K. Chesterton is reprinted by permission of The Bodley Head Ltd., London, and Dodd, Mead & Company, New York. Copyright 1908, 1935 by G. K. Chesterton.

'What I Believe' from *Two Cheers for Democracy* by E. M. Forster is reprinted by permission of Edward Arnold (Publishers) Ltd., London, and Harcourt, Brace & World, Inc., New York. Copyright 1951 by E. M. Forster.

'Oxford As I See It' from *My Discovery of England* by Stephen Leacock is reprinted by permission of The Bodley Head Ltd., London, and Dodd, Mead & Company, New York. Copyright 1922 by Dodd, Mead & Company, Inc.

'The Crime' from the book *And Even Now* by Max Beerbohm is reprinted by permission of William Heinemann Ltd., London, and E. P. Dutton & Co., Inc., New York. Copyright 1921 by E. P. Dutton & Co., Inc. Renewal 1949 by Max Beerbohm.

'How Should One Read a Book?' from *The Second Common Reader* by Virginia Woolf is reprinted by permission of The Hogarth Press Ltd., London, and Leonard Woolf, and Harcourt, Brace & World, Inc., New

Contents

Preface

It is not easy to say what an essay is. The word has been used to cover the tersely illustrated epigrams of Bacon and the digressive ruminations of Montaigne, the whimsical reflections of Lamb, the oracular insights of Emerson, and the ordered arguments of John Stuart Mill. Remembering its French origin in *essai*, perhaps one may call the essay simply an attempt to open out a subject.

Given such a latitude of meaning in the word, we have selected chapters from books as well as separately published essays in which subjects are explored with intelligence and writing skill. Our arrangement of material is mainly chronological yet also designed to provide the reader with illuminating comparisons and contrasts.

We have prepared this book for our students, but we hope that it will please anyone who enjoys ideas well expressed.

R. C.
C. K.

University of Saskatchewan
Saskatoon, Canada

JONATHAN SWIFT (1667–1745)

A Modest Proposal

FOR PREVENTING THE CHILDREN OF POOR
PEOPLE IN IRELAND, FROM BEING A BURDEN
TO THEIR PARENTS OR COUNTRY; AND FOR
MAKING THEM BENEFICIAL TO THE PUBLIC

It is a melancholy object to those who walk through this great town, or travel in the country, when they see the streets, the roads, and cabin doors crowded with beggars of the female sex, followed by three, four or six children, *all in rags*, and importuning every passenger for an alms. These mothers, instead of being able to work for their honest livelihood, are forced to employ all their time in strolling, to beg sustenance for their helpless infants, who, as they grow up, either turn thieves for want of work, or leave their dear native country to fight for the Pretender in Spain, or sell themselves to the Barbados.

I think it is agreed by all parties that this prodigious number of children in the arms, or on the backs, or at the heels of their mothers, and frequently of their fathers, is in the present deplorable state of the kingdom a very great additional grievance; and therefore whoever could find out a fair, cheap, and easy method of making these children sound and useful members of the commonwealth would deserve so well of the public as to have his statue set up for a preserver of the nation.

But my intention is very far from being confined to provide only for the children of professed beggars; it is of a much greater extent, and shall take in the whole number of infants at a certain age who are born of parents in effect as little able to support them as those who demand our charity in the streets.

As to my own part, having turned my thoughts, for many years, upon this important subject, and maturely weighed the several schemes of other projectors, I have always found them grossly mistaken in their computation. It is true a child, just dropped from its dam, may be supported by her milk for a solar year with little other nourishment, at most not above the value of two shillings, which the mother may certainly get, or the value in scraps, by her lawful occupation of begging: and it is exactly at one year old that I propose to provide for them, in such a manner as, instead of being a charge upon their parents, or the parish, or wanting food and raiment for the rest of their lives, they shall, on the contrary, contribute to the feeding and partly to the clothing of many thousands.

There is likewise another great advantage in my scheme, that it will prevent those voluntary abortions, and that horrid practice of women murdering their bastard children, alas, too frequent among us; sacrificing the poor innocent babes, I doubt, more to avoid the expense than the shame; which would move tears and pity in the most savage and inhuman breast.

The number of souls in Ireland being usually reckoned one million and a half, of these I calculate there may be about two hundred thousand couples whose wives are breeders; from which number I subtract thirty thousand couples who are able to maintain their own children, although I apprehend there cannot be so many under the present distresses of the kingdom; but this being granted, there will remain an hundred and seventy thousand breeders. I again subtract fifty thousand for those women who miscarry, or whose children die by accident or disease within the year. There only remain an hundred and twenty thousand children of poor parents, annually born: The question therefore is, how this number shall be reared, and provided for; which, as I have already said, under the present situation of affairs, is utterly impossible by all the methods hitherto proposed: for we can neither employ them in handicraft, or agriculture; we neither build houses (I mean in the country), nor cultivate land: they can very seldom pick up a livelihood by stealing until they arrive at six years old, except where they are of towardly parts; although, I confess they learn the rudiments much earlier, during which time they can however be properly looked upon only as *probationers;* as I have been informed by a principal gentleman in the County of Cavan, who protested to me that he never knew above one or two instances under the age of six, even in a part of the kingdom so renowned for the quickest proficiency in that art.

I am assured by our merchants that a boy or a girl, before twelve years old, is no saleable commodity, and even when they come to this age, they will not yield above three pounds, or three pounds and half a crown at most on the Exchange; which cannot turn to account either to the parents or kingdom, the charge of nutriment and rags having been at least four times that value.

I shall now therefore humbly propose my own thoughts, which I hope will not be liable to the least objection.

I have been assured by a very knowing American of my acquaintance in London, that a young healthy child well nursed is at a year old a most delicious, nourishing, and wholesome food, whether stewed, roasted, baked, or boiled; and I make no doubt that it will equally serve in a fricassee or a ragout.

I do therefore humbly offer it to public consideration, that of the hundred and twenty thousand children already computed, twenty thousand may be reserved for breed, whereof only one-fourth part to be males; which is more than we allow to sheep, black cattle, or swine; and my reason is that these children are seldom the fruits of marriage, a circumstance not much regarded by our savages, therefore one male will be sufficient to serve four females. That the remaining hundred thousand may at a year old be offered in sale to the persons of quality, and fortune, through the kingdom; always advising the mother to let them suck plentifully in the last month, so as to render them plump, and fat for a good table. A child will make two dishes at an entertainment for friends; and when the family dines alone, the fore- or hindquarter will make a reasonable dish, and seasoned with a little pepper or salt will be very good boiled on the fourth day, especially in winter.

I have reckoned upon a medium, that a child just born will weigh twelve pounds, and in a solar year if tolerably nursed increases to twenty-eight pounds.

I grant this food will be somewhat dear, and therefore very *proper for landlords*, who, as they have already devoured most of the parents, seem to have the best title to the children.

Infants' flesh will be in season throughout the year, but more plentiful in March, and a little before and after: for we are told by a grave author, an eminent French physician, that fish being a prolific diet, there are more children born in Roman Catholic countries about nine months after Lent than at any other season; therefore reckoning a year after Lent, the markets will be more glutted than usual, because the number of Popish infants is at least three to one in this king-dom; and therefore it will have one other collateral advantage by lessening the number of Papists among us.

I have already computed the charge of nursing a beggar's child (in which list I reckon all cottagers, labourers, and four-fifths of the farmers) to be about two shillings *per annum*, rags included; and I believe no gentleman would repine to give ten shillings for the carcass of a good fat child, which, as I have said, will make four dishes of excellent nutritive meat, when he hath only some particular friend or his own family to dine with him. Thus the squire will learn to be a good landlord, and grow popular among his tenants, the mother will have eight shillings net profit, and be fit for work until she produces another child.

Those who are more thrifty (*as I must confess the times*

require) may flay the carcass; the skin of which, artificially dressed, will make admirable gloves for ladies, and summer boots for fine gentlemen.

As to our City of Dublin, shambles may be appointed for this purpose, in the most convenient parts of it; and butchers we may be assured will not be wanting, although I rather recommend buying the children alive, and dressing them hot from the knife, as we do roasting pigs.

A very worthy person, a true lover of his country, and whose virtues I highly esteem, was lately pleased, in discoursing on this matter, to offer a refinement upon my scheme. He said that many gentlemen of this kingdom, having of late destroyed their deer, he conceived that the want of venison might be well supplied by the bodies of young lads and maidens, not exceeding fourteen years of age, nor under twelve; so great a number of both sexes in every country being now ready to starve, for want of work and service: and these to be disposed of by their parents if alive, or otherwise by their nearest relations. But with due deference to so excellent a friend, and so deserving a patriot, I cannot be altogether in his sentiments. For as to the males, my American acquaintance assured me from frequent experience that their flesh was generally tough and lean, like that of our schoolboys, by continual exercise, and their taste disagreeable, and to fatten them would not answer the charge. Then as to the females, it would, I think with humble submission, be a loss to the public, because they soon would become breeders themselves: And besides, it is not improbable that some scrupulous people might be apt to censure such a practice (although indeed very unjustly) as a little bordering upon cruelty; which, I confess, hath always been with me the strongest objection against any project, how well soever intended.

But in order to justify my friend, he confessed that this expedient was put into his head by the famous Psalmanazar, a native of the island Formosa, who came from thence to London, above twenty years ago, and in conversation told my friend that in his country when any young person happened

to be put to death, the executioner sold the carcass to persons
of quality, as a prime dainty; and that, in his time, the body
of a plump girl of fifteen, who was crucified for an attempt to
poison the emperor, was sold to his Imperial Majesty's Prime
Minister of State, and other great mandarins of the court, in
joints from the gibbet, at four hundred crowns. Neither indeed
can I deny that if the same use were made of several plump
young girls in this town, who, without one single groat to
their fortunes, cannot stir abroad without a chair, and appear
at a playhouse, and assemblies in foreign fineries, which they
never will pay for, the kingdom would not be the worse.

Some persons of a desponding spirit are in great concern
about that vast number of poor people, who are aged, dis-
eased, or maimed; and I have been desired to employ my
thoughts what course may be taken to ease the nation of so
grievous an encumbrance. But I am not in the least pain upon
that matter, because it is very well known that they are every
day dying, and rotting, by cold, and famine, and filth, and
vermin, as fast as can be reasonably expected. And as to the
younger labourers they are now in almost as hopeful a condition. They cannot get work, and consequently pine away for
want of nourishment, to a degree, that if at any time they are
accidentally hired to common labour, they have not strength
to perform it; and thus the country and themselves are in a
fair way of being soon delivered from the evils to come.

I have too long digressed, and therefore shall return to my
subject. I think the advantages by the proposal which I have
made are obvious and many, as well as of the highest importance.

For first, as I have already observed, it would greatly
lessen the number of Papists, with whom we are yearly overrun, being the principal breeders of the nation, as well as our
most dangerous enemies; and who stay at home on purpose
with a design to deliver the kingdom to the Pretender; hoping
to take their advantage by the absence of so many good
Protestants, who have chosen rather to leave their country

than stay at home, and pay tithes against their conscience to an idolatrous Episcopal curate.

Secondly, The poorer tenants will have something valuable of their own, which by law may be made liable to distress, and help to pay their landlord's rent, their corn and cattle being already seized, and *money a thing unknown*.

Thirdly, Whereas the maintenance of an hundred thousand children, from two years old, and upwards, cannot be computed at less than ten shillings apiece *per annum*, the nation's stock will be thereby increased fifty thousand pounds *per annum*; besides the profit of a new dish, introduced to the tables of all gentlemen of fortune in the kingdom, who have any refinement in taste; and the money will circulate among ourselves, the goods being entirely of our own growth and manufacture.

Fourthly, The constant breeders, besides the gain of eight shillings sterling *per annum*, by the sale of their children, will be rid of the charge of maintaining them after the first year.

Fifthly, This food would likewise bring great custom to taverns, where the vintners will certainly be so prudent as to procure the best receipts for dressing it to perfection, and consequently have their houses frequented by all the fine gentlemen, who justly value themselves upon their knowledge in good eating; and a skillful cook, who understands how to oblige his guests, will contrive to make it as expensive as they please.

Sixthly, This would be a great inducement to marriage, which all wise nations have either encouraged by rewards, or enforced by laws and penalties. It would increase the care and tenderness of mothers toward their children, when they were sure of a settlement for life, to the poor babes, provided in some sort by the public to their annual profit instead of expense. We should see an honest emulation among the married women, *which of them could bring the fattest child to the market*. Men would become as fond of their wives, during the time of their pregnancy, as they are now of their mares in foal, their cows in calf, or sows when they are ready to farrow; nor offer to beat or kick them (as it is too frequent a practice) for fear of a miscarriage.

Many other advantages might be enumerated. For instance, the addition of some thousand carcasses in our exportation of barrelled beef; the propagation of swine's flesh, and improvement in the art of making good bacon, so much wanted among us by the great destruction of pigs, too frequent at our tables, and are no way comparable in taste or magnificence to a well-grown, fat yearling child, which roasted whole will make a considerable figure at a Lord Mayor's feast, or any other public entertainment. But this and many others I omit, being studious of brevity.

Supposing that one thousand families in this city would be constant customers for infants' flesh, besides others who might have it at merry-meetings, particularly at weddings and christenings, I compute that Dublin would take off annually about twenty thousand carcasses, and the rest of the kingdom (where probably they will be sold somewhat cheaper) the remaining eighty thousand.

I can think of no one objection that will possibly be raised against this proposal, unless it should be urged that the number of people will be thereby much lessened in the kingdom. This I freely own, and it was indeed one principal design in offering it to the world. I desire the reader will observe, that I calculate my remedy *for this one individual Kingdom of Ireland, and for no other that ever was, is, or, I think, ever can be upon earth.* Therefore let no man talk to me of other expedients: *Of taxing our absentees at five shillings a pound: Of using neither clothes, nor household furniture, except what is of our own growth and manufacture: Of utterly rejecting the materials and instruments that promote foreign luxury: Of curing the expensiveness of pride, vanity, idleness, and gaming in our women: Of introducing a vein of parsimony, prudence, and temperance: Of learning to love our Country, wherein we differ even from* LAPLANDERS, *and the inhabitants of* TOPINAMBOO: *Of quitting our animosities and factions, nor act any longer like the Jews, who were murdering one another at the very moment their city was taken: Of being a little cautious not to sell our country and consciences for nothing: Of teaching landlords to have at least one degree of mercy toward their tenants.* Lastly, *of putting a spirit of honesty, industry, and skill into our shop-keepers, who, if a resolution could now be taken to buy our native goods, would immediately unite to cheat and exact upon us in the price, the measure, and the goodness; nor could ever yet be brought to make one fair proposal of just dealing, though often and earnestly invited to it.*

Therefore I repeat, let no man talk to me of these and the like expedients; until he hath at least a glimpse of hope that there will ever be some hearty and sincere attempt to put them in practice.

But as to myself, having been wearied out for many years with offering vain, idle, visionary thoughts, and at length utterly despairing of success, I fortunately fell upon this proposal, which as it is wholly new, so it hath something *solid* and *real*, of no expense and little trouble, full in our own power, and whereby we can incur no danger in *disobliging* ENGLAND. For this kind of commodity will not bear exportation, the flesh being of too tender a consistence to admit a long continuance in salt; *although perhaps I could name a country which would be glad to eat up our whole nation without it.*

After all I am not so violently bent upon my own opinion as to reject any offer, proposed by wise men, which shall be found equally innocent, cheap, easy, and effectual. But before something of that kind shall be advanced in contradiction to my scheme, and offering a better, I desire the author, or authors, will be pleased maturely to consider two points. First, as things now stand, how they will be able to find food and raiment for an hundred thousand useless mouths and backs. And secondly, there being a round million of creatures in human figure, throughout this kingdom, whose whole sub-sistence put into a common stock would leave them in debt two millions of pounds sterling; adding those, who are beggars by profession, to the bulk of farmers, cottagers, and labourers with their wives and children, who are beggars in effect; I desire those politicians, who dislike my overture, and may perhaps be so bold to attempt an answer, that they will first ask the parents of these mortals whether they would not at this day think it a great happiness to have been sold for food at a year old, in the manner I prescribe, and thereby have avoided such a perpetual scene of misfortunes as they have since gone through; by the oppression of landlords; the impossibility of paying rent without money or trade; the want of common sustenance, with neither house nor clothes to cover them from the inclemencies of the weather; and the most inevitable prospect of entailing the like, or greater miseries upon their breed forever.

I profess in the sincerity of my heart that I have not the least personal interest in endeavouring to promote this necessary work, having no other motive than the *public good of my country, by advancing our trade, providing for infants, relieving the poor, and giving some pleasure to the rich.* I have no children by which I can propose to get a single penny; the youngest being nine years old, and my wife past childbearing.

1729

JOHN STUART MILL (1806–1873)

On Liberty

(INTRODUCTORY CHAPTER)

The subject of this Essay is not the so-called Liberty of the Will, so unfortunately opposed to the misnamed doctrine of Philosophical Necessity; but Civil, or Social Liberty: the nature and limits of the power which can be legitimately exercised by society over the individual. A question seldom stated, and hardly ever discussed, in general terms, but which profoundly influences the practical controversies of the age by its latent presence, and is likely soon to make itself recognized as the vital question of the future. It is so far from being new, that, in a certain sense, it has divided mankind, almost from the remotest ages; but in the stage of progress into which the more civilized portions of the species have now entered, it presents itself under new conditions, and requires a different and more fundamental treatment.

The struggle between Liberty and Authority is the most conspicuous feature in the portions of history with which we are earliest familiar, particularly in that of Greece, Rome, and England. But in old times this contest was between subjects, or some classes of subjects, and the Government. By liberty, was meant protection against the tyranny of the political rulers. The rulers were conceived (except in some of the popular governments of Greece) as in a necessarily antagonistic position to the people whom they ruled. They consisted of a

governing One, or a governing tribe or caste, who derived
their authority from inheritance or conquest, who, at all
events, did not hold it at the pleasure of the governed, and
whose supremacy men did not venture, perhaps did not desire,
to contest, whatever precautions might be taken against its
oppressive exercise. Their power was regarded as necessary,
but also as highly dangerous; as a weapon which they would
attempt to use against their subjects, no less than against
external enemies. To prevent the weaker members of the
community from being preyed upon by innumerable vultures,
it was needful that there should be an animal of prey stronger
than the rest, commissioned to keep them down. But as the
king of the vultures would be no less bent upon preying on
the flock than any of the minor harpies, it was indispensable to
be in a perpetual attitude of defence against his beak and
claws. The aim, therefore, of patriots was to set limits to the
power which the ruler should be suffered to exercise over the
community; and this limitation was what they meant by
liberty. It was attempted in two ways. First, by obtaining a
recognition of certain immunities, called political liberties or
rights, which it was to be regarded as a breach of duty in the
ruler to infringe, and which, if he did infringe, specific resist-
ance, or general rebellion, was held to be justifiable. A second,
and generally a later expedient, was the establishment of
constitutional checks, by which the consent of the community, or of a body of some sort, supposed to represent its
interests, was made a necessary condition to some of the more
important acts of the governing power. To the first of these
modes of limitation, the ruling power, in most European
countries, was compelled, more or less, to submit. It was not
so with the second; and, to attain this, or when already in
some degree possessed, to attain it more completely, became
everywhere the principal object of the lovers of liberty. And
so long as mankind were content to combat one enemy by
another, and to be ruled by a master, on condition of being
guaranteed more or less efficaciously against his tyranny, they
did not carry their aspirations beyond this point.

A time, however, came, in the progress of human affairs, when men ceased to think it a necessity of nature that their governors should be an independent power, opposed in interest to themselves. It appeared to them much better that the various magistrates of the State should be their tenants or delegates, revocable at their pleasure. In that way alone, it seemed, could they have complete security that the powers of government would never be abused to their disadvantage. By degrees this new demand for elective and temporary rulers became the prominent object of the exertions of the popular party, wherever any such party existed; and superseded, to a considerable extent, the previous efforts to limit the power of rulers. As the struggle proceeded for making the ruling power emanate from the periodical choice of the ruled, some persons began to think that too much importance had been attached to the limitation of the power itself. *That* (it might seem) was a resource against rulers whose interests were habitually opposed to those of the people. What was now wanted was, that the rulers should be identified with the people; that their interest and will should be the interest and will of the nation. The nation did not need to be protected against its own will. There was no fear of its tyrannizing over itself. Let the rulers be effectually responsible to it, promptly removable by it, and it could afford to trust them with power of which it could itself dictate the use to be made. Their power was but the nation's own power, concentrated, and in a form convenient for exercise. This mode of thought, or rather perhaps of feeling, was common among the last generation of European liberalism, in the Continental section of which it still apparently predominates. Those who admit any limit to what a government may do, except in the case of such governments as they think ought not to exist, stand out as brilliant exceptions among the political thinkers of the Continent. A similar tone of sentiment might by this time have been prevalent in our own country, if the circumstances which for a time encouraged it, had continued unaltered.

But, in political and philosophical theories, as well as in

persons, success discloses faults and infirmities which failure might have concealed from observation. The notion, that the people have no need to limit their power over themselves, might seem axiomatic, when popular government was a thing only dreamed about, or read of as having existed at some distant period of the past. Neither was that notion necessarily disturbed by such temporary aberrations as those of the French Revolution, the worst of which were the work of a usurping few, and which, in any case, belonged, not to the permanent working of popular institutions, but to a sudden and convulsive outbreak against monarchical and aristocratic despotism. In time, however, a democratic republic came to occupy a large portion of the earth's surface, and made itself felt as one of the most powerful members of the community of nations; and elective and responsible government became subject to the observations and criticisms which wait upon a great existing fact. It was now perceived that such phrases as 'self-government', and 'the power of the people over themselves', do not express the true state of the case. The 'people' who exercise the power are not always the same people with those over whom it is exercised; and the 'self-government' spoken of is not the government of each by himself, but of each by all the rest. The will of the people, moreover, practically means the will of the most numerous or the most active *part* of the people; the majority, or those who succeed in making themselves accepted as the majority; the people, consequently, *may* desire to oppress a part of their number; and precautions are as much needed against this as against any other abuse of power. The limitation, therefore, of the power of government over individuals loses none of its importance when the holders of power are regularly accountable to the community, that is, to the strongest party therein. This view of things, recommending itself equally to the intelligence of thinkers and to the inclination of those important classes in European society to whose real or supposed interests democracy is adverse, has had no difficulty in establishing itself; and in political speculations 'the tyranny of the majority' is now generally included among the evils against which society requires to be on its guard.

Like other tyrannies, the tyranny of the majority was at first, and is still vulgarly, held in dread, chiefly as operating through the acts of the public authorities. But reflecting persons perceived that when society is itself the tyrant – society collectively, over the separate individuals who compose it – its means of tyrannizing are not restricted to the acts which it may do by the hands of its political functionaries. Society can and does execute its own mandates: and if it issues wrong mandates instead of right, or any mandates at all in things with which it ought not to meddle, it practises a social tyranny more formidable than many kinds of political oppression, since, though not usually upheld by such extreme penalties, it leaves fewer means of escape, penetrating much more deeply into the details of life, and enslaving the soul itself. Protection, therefore, against the tyranny of the magistrate is not enough: there needs protection also against the tyranny of the prevailing opinion and feeling; against the tendency of society to impose, by other means than civil penalties, its own ideas and practices as rules of conduct on those who dissent from them; to fetter the development, and, if possible, prevent the formation, of any individuality not in harmony with its ways, and compel all characters to fashion themselves upon the model of its own. There is a limit to the legitimate interference of collective opinion with individual independence: and to find that limit, and maintain it against encroachment, is as indispensable to a good condition of human affairs, as protection against political despotism.

But though this proposition is not likely to be contested in general terms, the practical question, where to place the limit – how to make the fitting adjustment between individual independence and social control – is a subject on which nearly everything remains to be done. All that makes existence valuable to any one, depends on the enforcement of restraints upon the actions of other people. Some rules of conduct, therefore, must be imposed, by law in the first place, and by

opinion on many things which are not fit subjects for the
operation of law. What these rules should be, is the principal
question in human affairs; but if we except a few of the most
obvious cases, it is one of those which least progress has been
made in resolving. No two ages, and scarcely any two countries, have decided it alike; and the decision of one age or
country is a wonder to another. Yet the people of any given
age and country no more suspect any difficulty in it, than if it
were a subject on which mankind had always been agreed.
The rules which obtain among themselves appear to them
self-evident and self-justifying. This all but universal illusion
is one of the examples of the magical influence of custom,
which is not only, as the proverb says, a second nature, but is
continually mistaken for the first. The effect of custom, in
preventing any misgiving respecting the rules of conduct which
mankind impose on one another, is all the more complete
because the subject is one on which it is not generally considered necessary that reasons should be given, either by one
person to others, or by each to himself. People are accustomed
to believe, and have been encouraged in the belief by some
who aspire to the character of philosophers, that their feelings, on subjects of this nature, are better than reasons, and
render reasons unnecessary. The practical principle which
guides them to their opinions on the regulation of human
conduct, is the feeling in each person's mind that everybody
should be required to act as he, and those with whom he sym-
pathizes, would like them to act. No one, indeed, acknowl-
edges to himself that his standard of judgment is his own
liking; but an opinion on a point of conduct, not supported
by reasons, can only count as one person's preference; and if
the reasons, when given, are a mere appeal to a similar
preference felt by other people, it is still only many people's
liking instead of one. To an ordinary man, however, his own
preference, thus supported, is not only a perfectly satisfactory
reason, but the only one he generally has for any of his notions
of morality, taste, or propriety, which are not expressly

written in his religious creed; and his chief guide in the inter-
pretation even of that. Men's opinions, accordingly, on what
is laudable or blamable, are affected by all the multifarious
causes which influence their wishes in regard to the conduct of
others, and which are as numerous as those which determine
their wishes on any other subject. Sometimes their reason –
at other times their prejudices or superstitions: often their
social affections, not seldom their antisocial ones, their envy
or jealousy, their arrogance or contemptuousness: but most
commonly their desires or fears for themselves – their legitimate or illegitimate self-interest. Wherever there is an ascendant class, a large portion of the morality of the country
emanates from its class interests, and its feelings of class
superiority. The morality between Spartans and Helots, between planters and negroes, between princes and subjects,
between nobles and roturiers, between men and women, has
been for the most part the creation of these class interests and
feelings: and the sentiments thus generated react in turn upon
the moral feelings of the members of the ascendant class, in
their relations among themselves. Where, on the other hand,
a class, formerly ascendant, has lost its ascendancy, or where
its ascendancy is unpopular, the prevailing moral sentiments
frequently bear the impress of an impatient dislike of superiority. Another grand determining principle of the rules of
conduct, both in act and forbearance, which have been enforced by law or opinion, has been the servility of mankind
towards the supposed preferences or aversions of their temporal masters or of their gods. This servility, though essentially
selfish, is not hypocrisy; it gives rise to perfectly genuine
sentiments of abhorrence; it made men burn magicians and
heretics. Among so many baser influences, the general and
obvious interests of society have of course had a share, and
a large one, in the reduction of the moral sentiments: less,
however, as a matter of reason, and on their own account,
than as a consequence of the sympathies and antipathies
which grew out of them: and sympathies and antipathies

which had little or nothing to do with the interests of society, have made themselves felt in the establishment of moralities with quite as great force.

The likings and dislikings of society, or of some powerful portion of it, are thus the main thing which has practically determined the rules laid down for general observance, under the penalties of law or opinion. And in general, those who have been in advance of society in thought and feeling, have left this condition of things unassailed in principle, however they may have come into conflict with it in some of its details. They have occupied themselves rather in inquiring what things society ought to like or dislike, than in questioning whether its likings or dislikings should be a law to individuals. They preferred endeavouring to alter the feelings of mankind on the particular points on which they were themselves heretical, rather than make common cause in defence of freedom, with heretics generally. The only case in which the higher ground has been taken on principle and maintained with consistency, by any but an individual here and there, is that of religious belief: a case instructive in many ways, and not least so as forming a most striking instance of the fallibility of what is called the moral sense: for the *odium theologicum*, in a sincere bigot, is one of the most unequivocal cases of moral feeling. Those who first broke the yoke of what called itself the Universal Church, were in general as little willing to permit difference of religious opinion as that church itself. But when the heat of the conflict was over, without giving a complete victory to any party, and each church or sect was reduced to limit its hopes to retaining possession of the ground it already occupied; minorities, seeing that they had no chance of becoming majorities, were under the necessity of pleading to those whom they could not convert, for permission to differ. It is accordingly on this battlefield, almost solely, that the rights of the individual against society have been asserted on broad grounds of principle, and the claim of society to exercise authority over dissentients openly controverted. The great writers to whom the world owes what religious liberty it possesses, have mostly asserted freedom of conscience as an indefeasible right, and denied absolutely that a human being is accountable to others for his religious belief. Yet so natural to mankind is intolerance in whatever they really care about, that religious freedom has hardly anywhere been practically realized, except where religious indifference, which dislikes to have its peace disturbed by theological quarrels, has added its weight to the scale. In the minds of almost all religious persons, even in the most tolerant countries, the duty of toleration is admitted with tacit reserves. One person will bear with dissent in matters of church government, but not of dogma; another can tolerate everybody, short of a Papist, or a Unitarian; another every one who believes in a revealed religion; a few extend their charity a little further, but stop at the belief in a God and in a future state. Wherever the sentiment of the majority is still genuine and intense, it is found to have abated little of its claim to be obeyed.

In England, from the peculiar circumstances of our political history, though the yoke of opinion is perhaps heavier, that of law is lighter, than in most other countries of Europe; and there is considerable jealousy of direct interference, by the legislative or the executive power, with private conduct; not so much from any just regard for the independence of the individual, as from the still subsisting habit of looking on the government as representing an opposite interest to the public. The majority have not yet learnt to feel the power of the government their power, or its opinions their opinions. When they do so, individual liberty will probably be as much exposed to invasion from the government, as it already is from public opinion. But, as yet, there is a considerable amount of feeling ready to be called forth against any attempt of the law to control individuals in things in which they have not hitherto been accustomed to be controlled by it; and this with very little discrimination as to whether the matter is, or is not, within the legitimate sphere of legal control; insomuch that the feeling, highly salutary on the whole, is perhaps quite as often misplaced as well grounded in the particular instances

of its application. There is, in fact, no recognized principle
by which the propriety or impropriety of government interference is customarily tested. People decide according to their
personal preferences. Some, whenever they see any good to be
done, or evil to be remedied, would willingly instigate the
government to undertake the business; while others prefer to
bear almost any amount of social evil, rather than add one to
the departments of human interests amenable to govern-
mental control. And men range themselves on one or the
other side in any particular case, according to this general
direction of their sentiments; or according to the degree of
interest which they feel in the particular thing which it is
proposed that the government should do, or according to the
belief they entertain that the government would, or would not,
do it in the manner they prefer; but very rarely on account of
any opinion to which they consistently adhere, as to what
things are fit to be done by a government. And it seems to me
that in consequence of this absence of rule or principle, one
side is at present as often wrong as the other; the interference
of government is, with about equal frequency, improperly
invoked and improperly condemned.

The object of this Essay is to assert one very simple principle,
as entitled to govern absolutely the dealings of society with
the individual in the way of compulsion and control, whether
the means used be physical force in the form of legal penalties,
or the moral coercion of public opinion. That principle is,
that the sole end for which mankind are warranted, indi-
vidually or collectively, in interfering with the liberty of action
of any of their number, is self-protection. That the only
purpose for which power can be rightfully exercised over
any member of a civilized community, against his will, is to
prevent harm to others. His own good, either physical or
moral, is not a sufficient warrant. He cannot rightfully be
compelled to do or forbear because it will be better for him to
do so, because it will make him happier, because, in the
opinions of others, to do so would be wise, or even right.

These are good reasons for remonstrating with him, or reasoning with him, or persuading him, or entreating him, but not for compelling him, or visiting him with any evil in case he do otherwise. To justify that, the conduct from which it is desired to deter him must be calculated to produce evil to someone else. The only part of the conduct of any one, for which he is amenable to society, is that which concerns others. In the part which merely concerns himself, his independence is, of right, absolute. Over himself, over his own body and mind, the individual is sovereign.

It is, perhaps, hardly necessary to say that this doctrine is meant to apply to human beings in the maturity of their faculties. We are not speaking of children, or of young persons below the age which the law may fix as that of manhood or womanhood. Those who are still in a state to require being taken care of by others, must be protected against their own actions as well as against external injury. For the same reason, we may leave out of consideration those backward states of society in which the race itself may be considered as in its nonage. The early difficulties in the way of spontaneous progress are so great, that there is seldom any choice of means for overcoming them; and a ruler full of the spirit of improvement is warranted in the use of any expedients that will attain an end, perhaps otherwise unattainable. Despotism is a legitimate mode of government in dealing with barbarians, provided the end be their improvement, and the means justified by actually effecting that end. Liberty, as a principle, has no application to any state of things anterior to the time when mankind have become capable of being improved by free and equal discussion. Until then, there is nothing for them but implicit obedience to an Akbar or a Charlemagne, if they are so fortunate as to find one. But as soon as mankind have attained the capacity of being guided to their own improvement by conviction or persuasion (a period long since reached in all nations with whom we need here concern ourselves), compulsion, either in the direct form or in that of pains and penalties for non-compliance, is no longer admissible as a means to their own good, and justifiable only for the security of others.

It is proper to state that I forego any advantage which could be derived to my argument from the idea of abstract right, as a thing independent of utility. I regard utility as the ultimate appeal on all ethical questions; but it must be utility in the largest sense, grounded on the permanent interests of a man as a progressive being. Those interests, I contend, authorize the subjection of individual spontaneity to external control, only in respect to those actions of each, which concern the interest of other people. If any one does an act hurtful to others, there is a *prima facie* case for punishing him, by law, or, where legal penalties are not safely applicable, by general disapprobation. There are also many positive acts for the benefit of others, which he may rightfully be compelled to perform; such as to give evidence in a court of justice; to bear his fair share in the common defence, or in any other joint work necessary to the interest of the society of which he enjoys the protection; and to perform certain acts of individual beneficence, such as saving a fellow creature's life, or interposing to protect the defenceless against ill-usage, things which whenever it is obviously a man's duty to do, he may rightfully be made responsible for not doing. A person may cause evil to others not only by his actions but by his inaction, and in either case he is justly accountable to them for the injury. The latter case, it is true, requires a much more cautious exercise of compulsion than the former. To make any one answerable for doing evil to others is the rule; to make him answerable for not preventing evil is, comparatively speaking, the exception. Yet there are many cases clear enough and grave enough to justify that exception. In all things which regard the external relations of the individual, he is *de jure* amenable to those whose interests are concerned, and, if need be, to society as their protector. There are often good reasons for not holding him to the responsibility; but these reasons must arise from the special expediencies of the case: either because it is a kind of case in which he is on the whole likely to act better, when left to his own discretion, than when controlled in any way in which society have it in their power to control him; or because the attempt to exercise control would produce other evils, greater than those which it would prevent. When such reasons as these preclude the enforcement of responsibility, the conscience of the agent himself should step into the vacant judgment seat, and protect those interests of others which have no external protection; judging himself all the more rigidly, because the case does not admit of his being made accountable to the judgment of his fellow creatures.

But there is a sphere of action in which society, as distinguished from the individual, has, if any, only an indirect interest; comprehending all that portion of a person's life and conduct which affects only himself, or if it also affects others, only with their free, voluntary, and undeceived consent and participation. When I say only himself, I mean directly, and in the first instance; for whatever affects himself, may affect others through himself; and the objection which may be grounded on this contingency, will receive consideration in the sequel. This, then, is the appropriate region of human liberty. It comprises, first, the inward domain of consciousness; demanding liberty of conscience in the most comprehensive sense; liberty of thought and feeling; absolute freedom of opinion and sentiment on all subjects, practical or speculative, scientific, moral, or theological. The liberty of expressing and publishing opinions may seem to fall under a different principle, since it belongs to that part of the conduct of an individual which concerns other people; but, being almost of as much importance as the liberty of thought itself, and resting in great part on the same reasons, is practically inseparable from it. Secondly, the principle requires liberty of tastes and pursuits; of framing the plan of our life to suit our own character; of doing as we like, subject to such consequences as may follow: without impediment from our fellow creatures, so long as what we do does not harm them, even though they should think our conduct foolish, perverse, or wrong. Thirdly, from this liberty of each individual, follows the liberty, within the same limits, of combination among individuals; freedom to unite, for any purpose not involving harm to others: the persons combining being supposed to be of full age, and not forced or deceived.

No society in which these liberties are not, on the whole, respected, is free, whatever may be its form of government; and none is completely free in which they do not exist absolute and unqualified. The only freedom which deserves the name, is that of pursuing our own good in our own way, so long as we do not attempt to deprive others of theirs, or impede their efforts to obtain it. Each is the proper guardian of his own health, whether bodily, *or* mental and spiritual. Mankind are greater gainers by suffering each other to live as seems good to themselves, than by compelling each to live as seems good to the rest.

Though this doctrine is anything but new, and, to some persons, may have the air of a truism, there is no doctrine which stands more directly opposed to the general tendency of existing opinion and practice. Society has expended fully as much effort in the attempt (according to its lights) to compel people to conform to its notions of personal as of social excellence. The ancient commonwealths thought themselves entitled to practise, and the ancient philosophers countenanced, the regulation of every part of private conduct by public authority, on the ground that the State had a deep interest in the whole bodily and mental discipline of every one of its citizens; a mode of thinking which may have been admissible in small republics surrounded by powerful enemies, in constant peril of being subverted by foreign attack or internal commotion, and to which even a short interval of relaxed energy and self-command might so easily be fatal that they could not afford to wait for the salutary permanent effects of freedom. In the modern world, the greater size of political communities, and, above all, the separation between spiritual and temporal authority (which placed the direction of men's consciences in other hands than those which controlled their worldly affairs), prevented so great an interference by law in the details of private life; but the engines of moral repression have been wielded more strenuously against divergence from the reigning opinion in self-regarding, than even in social matters; religion, the most powerful of the elements which have entered into the formation of moral feeling, having almost always been governed either by the ambition of a hierarchy, seeking control over every department of human conduct, or by the spirit of Puritanism. And some of those modern reformers who have placed themselves in strongest opposition to the religions of the past, have been noway behind either churches or sects in their assertion of the right of spiritual domination: M. Comte, in particular, whose social system, as unfolded in his *Système de Politique Positive*, aims at establishing (though by moral more than by legal appliances) a despotism of society over the individual, surpassing anything contemplated in the political ideal of the most rigid disciplinarian among the ancient philosophers.

Apart from the peculiar tenets of individual thinkers, there is also in the world at large an increasing inclination to stretch unduly the powers of society over the individual, both by the force of opinion and even by that of legislation; and as the tendency of all the changes taking place in the world is to strengthen society, and diminish the power of the individual, this encroachment is not one of the evils which tend spontaneously to disappear, but, on the contrary, to grow more and more formidable. The disposition of mankind, whether as rulers or as fellow citizens, to impose their own opinions and inclinations as a rule of conduct on others, is so energetically supported by some of the best and by some of the worst feelings incident to human nature, that it is hardly ever kept under restraint by anything but want of power; and as the power is not declining, but growing, unless a strong barrier of moral conviction can be raised against the mischief, we must expect, in the present circumstances of the world, to see it increase.

It will be convenient for the argument, if, instead of at once entering upon the general thesis, we confine ourselves in the first instance to a single branch of it, on which the principle here stated is, if not fully, yet to a certain point, recognized by the current opinions. This one branch is the Liberty of Thought: from which it is impossible to separate the cognate liberty of speaking and of writing. Although these liberties, to some considerable amount, form part of the political morality of all countries which profess religious toleration and free institutions, the grounds, both philosophical and practical, on which they rest, are perhaps not so familiar to the general mind, nor so thoroughly appreciated by many even of the leaders of opinion, as might have been expected. Those grounds, when rightly understood, are of much wider application than to only one division of the subject, and a thorough consideration of this part of the question will be found the best introduction to the remainder. Those to whom nothing which I am about to say will be new, may therefore, I hope, excuse me, if on a subject which for now three centuries has been so often discussed, I venture on one discussion more.

1859

G. K. CHESTERTON (1874–1936)

The Flag of the World

When I was a boy there were two curious men running about who were called the optimist and the pessimist. I constantly used the words myself, but I cheerfully confess that I never had any very special idea of what they meant. The only thing which might be considered evident was that they could not mean what they said; for the ordinary verbal explanation was that the optimist thought this world as good as it could be, while the pessimist thought it as bad as it could be. Both these statements being obviously raving nonsense, one had to cast about for other explanations. An optimist could not mean a man who thought everything right and nothing wrong. For that is meaningless; it is like calling everything right and nothing left. Upon the whole, I came to the conclusion that the optimist thought everything good except the pessimist, and that the pessimist thought everything bad, except himself. It would be unfair to omit altogether from the list the mysterious but suggestive definition said to have been given by a little girl, 'An optimist is a man who looks after your eyes, and a pessimist is a man who looks after your feet.' I am not sure that this is not the best definition of all. There is even a sort of allegorical truth in it. For there might, perhaps, be a profitable distinction drawn between that more dreary thinker who thinks merely of our contact with the earth from moment to moment, and that happier thinker who considers rather our primary power of vision and of choice of road.

But there is a deep mistake in this alternative of the optimist and the pessimist. The assumption of it is that a man criticizes this world as if he were house-hunting, as if he were being shown over a new suite of apartments. If a man came to this world from some other world in full possession of his powers he might discuss whether the advantage of midsummer woods made up for the disadvantage of mad dogs, just as a man looking for lodgings might balance the presence of a telephone against the absence of a sea view. But no man is in that position. A man belongs to this world before he begins to ask if it is nice to belong to it. He has fought for the flag, and often won heroic victories for the flag long before he has ever enlisted. To put shortly what seems the essential matter, he has a loyalty long before he has any admiration.

In the last chapter it has been said that the primary feeling that this world is strange and yet attractive is best expressed in fairy tales. The reader may, if he likes, put down the next stage to that bellicose and even jingo literature which commonly comes next in the history of a boy. We all owe much sound morality to the penny dreadfuls. Whatever the reason, it seemed and still seems to me that our attitude towards life can be better expressed in terms of a kind of military loyalty than in terms of criticism and approval. My acceptance of the universe is not optimism, it is more like patriotism. It is a matter of primary loyalty. The world is not a lodging-house at Brighton, which we are to leave because it is miserable. It is the fortress of our family, with the flag flying on the turret, and the more miserable it is the less we should leave it. The point is not that this world is too sad to love or too glad not to love; the point is that when you do love a thing, its gladness is a reason for loving it, and its sadness a reason for loving it more. All optimistic thoughts about England and all pessimistic thoughts about her are alike reasons for the English patriot. Similarly, optimism and pessimism are alike arguments for the cosmic patriot.

Let us suppose we are confronted with a desperate thing – say Pimlico. If we think what is really best for Pimlico we shall find the thread of thought leads to the throne or the mystic and the arbitrary. It is not enough for a man to disapprove of Pimlico: in that case he will merely cut his throat or move to Chelsea. Nor, certainly, is it enough for a man to approve of Pimlico: for then it will remain Pimlico, which would be awful. The only way out of it seems to be for somebody to love Pimlico: to love it with a transcendental tie and without any earthly reason. If there arose a man who loved Pimlico, then Pimlico would rise into ivory towers and golden pinnacles; Pimlico would attire herself as a woman does when she is loved. For decoration is not given to hide horrible things; but to decorate things already adorable. A mother does not give her child a blue bow because he is so ugly without it. A lover does not give a girl a necklace to hide her neck. If men loved Pimlico as mothers love children, arbitrarily, because it is *theirs*, Pimlico in a year or two might be fairer than Florence. Some readers will say that this is a mere fantasy. I answer that this is the actual history of mankind. This, as a fact, is how cities did grow great. Go back to the darkest roots of civilization and you will find them knotted round some sacred stone or encircling some sacred well. People first paid honour to a spot and afterwards gained glory for it. Men did not love Rome because she was great. She was great because they had loved her.

The eighteenth-century theories of the social contract have been exposed to much clumsy criticism in our time; in so far as they meant that there is at the back of all historic government an idea of content and co-operation, they were demonstrably right. But they really were wrong in so far as they suggested that men had ever aimed at order or ethics directly by a conscious exchange of interests. Morality did not begin by one man saying to another,'I will not hit you if you do not hit me'; there is no trace of such a transaction. There *is* a trace of both men having said, 'We must not hit each other in the holy place.' They gained their morality by guarding their religion. They did not cultivate courage. They fought for the shrine, and found they had become courageous. They did not cultivate cleanliness. They purified themselves for the altar, and found that they were clean. The history of the Jews is the only early document known to most Englishmen, and the facts can be judged sufficiently from that. The Ten Commandments which have been found substantially common to mankind were merely military commands; a code of regimental orders, issued to protect a certain ark across a certain desert. Anarchy was evil because it endangered the sanctity. And only when they made a holy day for God did they find they had made a holiday for men. If it be granted that this primary devotion to a place or thing is a source of creative energy, we can pass on to a very peculiar fact. Let us reiterate for an instant that the only right optimism is a sort of universal patriotism. What is the matter with the pessimist? I think it can be stated by saying that he is the cosmic anti-patriot. And what is the matter with the anti-patriot? I think it can be stated, without undue bitterness, by saying that he is the candid friend. And what is the matter with the candid friend? There we strike the rock of real life and immutable human nature.

I venture to say that what is bad in the candid friend is simply that he is not candid. He is keeping something back – his own gloomy pleasure in saying unpleasant things. He has a secret desire to hurt, not merely to help. This is certainly, I think, what makes a certain sort of anti-patriot irritating to healthy citizens. I do not speak (of course) of the anti-patriotism which only irritates feverish stockbrokers and gushing actresses; that is only patriotism speaking plainly. A man who says that no patriot should attack the Boer War until it is over is not worth answering intelligently; he is saying that no good son should warn his mother off a cliff until she has fallen over it. But there is an anti-patriot who honestly angers honest men, and the explanation of him is, I think, what I have suggested: he is the uncandid candid friend; the man who says, 'I am sorry to say we are ruined', and is not sorry at all. And he may be said, without rhetoric, to be a traitor; for he is using that ugly knowledge which was allowed him to strengthen the army, to discourage people from joining it. Because he is allowed to be pessimistic as a military adviser he is being pessimistic as a recruiting sergeant. Just in the same way the pessimist (who is the cosmic anti-patriot) uses the freedom that life allows to her counsellors to lure away the people from her flag. Granted that he states only facts, it is still essential to know what are his emotions, what is his motive. It may be that twelve hundred men in Tottenham are down with smallpox; but we want to know whether this is stated by some great philosopher who wants to curse the gods, or only by some common clergyman who wants to help the men.

The evil of the pessimist is, then, not that he chastises gods and men, but that he does not love what he chastises – he has not this primary and supernatural loyalty to things. What is the evil of the man commonly called an optimist? Obviously, it is felt that the optimist, wishing to defend the honour of this world, will defend the indefensible. He is the jingo of the universe; he will say, 'My cosmos, right or wrong.' He will be less inclined to the reform of things; more inclined to a sort of front-bench official answer to all attacks, soothing every one with assurances. He will not wash the world, but whitewash the world. All this (which is true of a type of optimist) leads us to the one really interesting point of psychology, which could not be explained without it.

We say there must be a primal loyalty to life: the only question is, shall it be a natural or a supernatural loyalty? If you like to put it so, shall it be a reasonable or an unreasonable loyalty? Now, the extraordinary thing is that the bad optimism (the whitewashing, the weak defence of everything) comes in with the reasonable optimism. Rational optimism leads to stagnation: it is irrational optimism that leads to reform. Let me explain by using once more the parallel of patriotism. The man who is most likely to ruin the place he loves is exactly the man who loves it with a reason. The man who will improve the place is the man who loves it without a reason. If a man loves some feature of Pimlico (which seems

unlikely), he may find himself defending that feature against
Pimlico itself. But if he simply loves Pimlico itself, he may lay
it waste and turn it into the New Jerusalem. I do not deny
that reform may be excessive; I only say that it is the mystic
patriot who reforms. Mere jingo self-contentment is commonest among those who have some pedantic reason for their
patriotism. The worst jingoes do not love England, but a
theory of England. If we love England for being an empire,
we may overrate the success with which we rule the Hindoos.
But if we love it only for being a nation, we can face all events:
for it would be a nation even if the Hindoos ruled us. Thus
also only those will permit their patriotism to falsify history
whose patriotism depends on history. A man who loves England for being English will not mind how she arose. But a man
who loves England for being Anglo-Saxon may go against all
facts for his fancy. He may end (like Carlyle and Freeman) by
maintaining that the Norman Conquest was a Saxon Conquest.
He may end in utter unreason – because he has a reason. A
man who loves France for being military will palliate the
army of 1870. But a man who loves France for being France
will improve the army of 1870. This is exactly what the French
have done, and France is a good instance of the working para-
dox. Nowhere else is patriotism more purely abstract and
arbitrary, and nowhere else is reform more drastic and sweeping. The more transcendental is your patriotism, the more
practical are your politics.

Perhaps the most everyday instance of this point is in the
case of women, and their strange and strong loyalty. Some
stupid people started the idea that because women obviously
back up their own people through everything, therefore women
are blind and do not see anything. They can hardly have
known any women. The same women who are ready to defend
their men through thick and thin are (in their personal intercourse with the man) almost morbidly lucid about the thinness
of his excuses or the thickness of his head. A man's friend
likes him but leaves him as he is: his wife loves him and is
always trying to turn him into somebody else. Women who

are utter mystics in their creed are utter cynics in their criticism. Thackeray expressed this well when he made Pendennis' mother, who worshipped her son as a god, yet assume that he would go wrong as a man. She underrated his virtue, though she overrated his value. The devotee is entirely free to criticize; the fanatic can safely be a sceptic. Love is not blind; that is the last thing it is. Love is bound; and the more it is bound the less it is blind.

This at least had come to be my position about all that was called optimism, pessimism, and improvement. Before any cosmic act of reform we must have a cosmic oath of allegiance. A man must be interested in life, then he could be disinterested in his views of it. 'My son give me thy heart'; the heart must be fixed on the right thing: the moment we have a fixed heart we have a free hand. I must pause to anticipate an obvious criticism. It will be said that a rational person accepts the world as mixed of good and evil with a decent satisfaction and a decent endurance. But this is exactly the attitude which I maintain to be defective. It is, I know, very common in this age; it was perfectly put in those quiet lines of Matthew Arnold which are more piercingly blasphemous than the shrieks of Schopenhauer –

> *Enough we live: – and if a life,*
> *With large results so little rife,*
> *Though bearable, seem hardly worth*
> *This pomp of worlds, this pain of birth.*

I know this feeling fills our epoch, and I think it freezes our epoch. For our Titanic purposes of faith and revolution, what we need is not the cold acceptance of the world as a compromise, but some way in which we can heartily hate and heartily love it. We do not want joy and anger to neutralize each other and produce a surly contentment; we want a fiercer delight and a fiercer discontent. We have to feel the universe at once as an ogre's castle, to be stormed, and yet as our own cottage, to which we can return at evening.

No one doubts that an ordinary man can get on with this

world: but we demand not strength enough to get on with it, but strength enough to get it on. Can he hate it enough to change it, and yet love it enough to think it worth changing? Can he look up at its colossal good without once feeling acquiescence? Can he look up at its colossal evil without once feeling despair? Can he, in short, be at once not only a pessimist and an optimist, but a fanatical pessimist and a fanatical optimist? Is he enough of a pagan to die for the world, and enough of a Christian to die to it? In this combination, I maintain, it is the rational optimist who fails, the irrational optimist who succeeds. He is ready to smash the whole universe for the sake of itself.

I put these things not in their mature logical sequence, but as they came: and this view was cleared and sharpened by an accident of the time. Under the lengthening shadow of Ibsen, an argument arose whether it was not a very nice thing to murder one's self. Grave moderns told us that we must not even say 'poor fellow', of a man who had blown his brains out, since he was an enviable person, and had only blown them out because of their exceptional excellence. Mr. William Archer even suggested that in the golden age there would be penny-in-the-slot machines by which a man could kill himself for a penny. In all this I found myself utterly hostile to many who called themselves liberal and humane. Not only is suicide a sin, it is the sin. It is the ultimate and absolute evil, the refusal to take an interest in existence; the refusal to take the oath of loyalty to life. The man who kills a man, kills a man. The man who kills himself, kills all men; as far as he is concerned he wipes out the world. His act is worse (symbolically considered) than any rape or dynamite outrage. For it destroys all buildings: it insults all women. The thief is satisfied with diamonds; but the suicide is not: that is his crime. He cannot be bribed, even by the blazing stones of the Celestial City. The thief compliments the things he steals, if not the owner of them. But the suicide insults everything on earth by not stealing it. He defiles every flower by refusing to live for its sake. There is not a tiny creature in the cosmos at whom his death is not a sneer. When a man hangs himself on a tree, the leaves might fall off in anger and the birds fly away in fury: for each has received a personal affront. Of course there may be pathetic emotional excuses for the act. There often are for rape, and there almost always are for dynamite. But if it comes to clear ideas and the intelligent meaning of things, then there is much more rational and philosophic truth in the burial at the crossroads and the stake driven through the body, than in Mr. Archer's suicidal automatic machines. There is a meaning in burying the suicide apart. The man's crime is different from other crimes – for it makes even crimes impossible.

1908

E. M. FORSTER (b.1879)

What I Believe

I do not believe in Belief. But this is an age of faith, and there are so many militant creeds that, in self-defence, one has to formulate a creed of one's own. Tolerance, good temper and sympathy are no longer enough in a world which is rent by religious and racial persecution, in a world where ignorance rules, and science, who ought to have ruled, plays the subservient pimp. Tolerance, good temper and sympathy – they are what matter really, and if the human race is not to collapse they must come to the front before long. But for the moment they are not enough, their action is no stronger than a flower, battered beneath a military jack-boot. They want stiffening, even if the process coarsens them. Faith, to my mind, is a stiffening process, a sort of mental starch, which ought to be applied as sparingly as possible. I dislike the stuff. I do not believe in it, for its own sake, at all. Herein I probably differ from most people, who believe in Belief, and are only sorry they cannot swallow even more than they do. My law-givers are Erasmus and Montaigne, not Moses and St. Paul. My temple stands not upon Mount Moriah but in that Elysian Field where even the immoral are admitted. My motto is: 'Lord, I disbelieve – help thou my unbelief.'

I have, however, to live in an Age of Faith – the sort of epoch I used to hear praised when I was a boy. It is extremely unpleasant really. It is bloody in every sense of the word. And I have to keep my end up in it. Where do I start?

With personal relationships. Here is something comparatively solid in a world full of violence and cruelty. Not absolutely solid, for Psychology has split and shattered the idea of
a 'Person', and has shown that there is something incalculable
in each of us, which may at any moment rise to the surface and
destroy our normal balance. We don't know what we are like.
We can't know what other people are like. How, then, can we
put any trust in personal relationships, or cling to them in the
gathering political storm? In theory we cannot. But in practice
we can and do. Though A is not unchangeably A or B unchangeably B, there can still be love and loyalty between the
two. For the purpose of living one has to assume that the
personality is solid, and the 'self' is an entity, and to ignore all
contrary evidence. And since to ignore evidence is one of the
characteristics of faith, I certainly can proclaim that I believe
in personal relationships.

Starting from them, I get a little order into the contemporary chaos. One must be fond of people and trust them if one
is not to make a mess of life, and it is therefore essential that
they should not let one down. They often do. The moral of
which is that I must, myself, be as reliable as possible, and
this I try to be. But reliability is not a matter of contract – that
is the main difference between the world of personal relationships and the world of business relationships. It is a matter for
the heart, which signs no documents. In other words, reliability is impossible unless there is a natural warmth. Most men
possess this warmth, though they often have bad luck and get
chilled. Most of them, even when they are politicians, *want* to
keep faith. And one can, at all events, show one's own little
light here, one's own poor little trembling flame, with the
knowledge that it is not the only light that is shining in the
darkness, and not the only one which the darkness does not
comprehend. Personal relations are despised today. They are
regarded as bourgeois luxuries, as products of a time of fair
weather which is now past, and we are urged to get rid of
them, and to dedicate ourselves to some movement or cause
instead. I hate the idea of causes, and if I had to choose be-

tween betraying my country and betraying my friend, I hope
I should have the guts to betray my country. Such a choice
may scandalize the modern reader, and he may stretch out his
patriotic hand to the telephone at once and ring up the police.
It would not have shocked Dante, though. Dante places
Brutus and Cassius in the lowest circle of Hell because they
had chosen to betray their friend Julius Caesar rather than
their country Rome. Probably one will not be asked to make
such an agonizing choice. Still, there lies at the back of every
creed something terrible and hard for which the worshipper
may one day be required to suffer, and there is even a terror
and a hardness in this creed of personal relationships, urbane
and mild though it sounds. Love and loyalty to an individual
can run counter to the claims of the State. When they do –
down with the State, say I, which means that the State would
down me.

This brings me along to Democracy, 'even Love, the Beloved
Republic, which feeds upon Freedom and lives'. Democracy
is not a Beloved Republic really, and never will be. But it is
less hateful than other contemporary forms of government,
and to that extent it deserves our support. It does start from
the assumption that the individual is important, and that all
types are needed to make a civilization. It does not divide its
citizens into the bossers and the bossed – as an efficiency-
régime tends to do. The people I admire most are those who
are sensitive and want to create something or discover something, and do not see life in terms of power, and such people
get more of a chance under a democracy than elsewhere. They
found religions, great or small, or they produce literature and
art, or they do disinterested scientific research, or they may be
what is called 'ordinary people', who are creative in their
private lives, bring up their children decently, for instance, or
help their neighbours. All these people need to express themselves; they cannot do so unless society allows them liberty to
do so, and the society which allows them most liberty is a
democracy.

Democracy has another merit. It allows criticism, and if

there is not public criticism there are bound to be hushed-up scandals. That is why I believe in the Press, despite all its lies and vulgarity, and why I believe in Parliament. Parliament is often sneered at because it is a Talking Shop. I believe in it *because* it is a talking shop. I believe in the Private Member who makes himself a nuisance. He gets snubbed and is told that he is cranky or ill-informed, but he does expose abuses which would otherwise never have been mentioned, and very often an abuse gets put right just by being mentioned. Occasionally, too, a well-meaning public official starts losing his head in the cause of efficiency, and thinks himself God Almighty. Such officials are particularly frequent in the Home Office. Well, there will be questions about them in Parliament sooner or later, and then they will have to mind their steps. Whether Parliament is either a representative body or an efficient one is questionable, but I value it because it criticizes and talks, and because its chatter gets widely reported.

So Two cheers for Democracy: one because it admits variety and two because it permits criticism. Two cheers are quite enough: there is no occasion to give three. Only Love the Beloved Republic deserves that.

What about Force, though? While we are trying to be sensitive and advanced and affectionate and tolerant, an unpleasant question pops up: does not all society rest upon force? If a government cannot count upon the police and the army, how can it hope to rule? And if an individual gets knocked on the head or sent to a labour camp, of what significance are his opinions?

This dilemma does not worry me as much as it does some. I realize that all society rests upon force. But all the great creative actions, all the decent human relations, occur during the intervals when force has not managed to come to the front. These intervals are what matter. I want them to be as frequent and as lengthy as possible, and I call them 'civilization'. Some people idealize force and pull it into the foreground and worship it, instead of keeping it in the background as long as possible. I think they make a mistake, and I think that their

opposites, the mystics, err even more when they declare that
force does not exist. I believe that it exists, and that one of our
jobs is to prevent it from getting out of its box. It gets out
sooner or later, and then it destroys us and all the lovely things
which we have made. But it is not out all the time, for the
fortunate reason that the strong are so stupid. Consider their
conduct for a moment in the Niebelung's Ring. The giants
there have the guns, or in other words the gold; but they do
nothing with it, they do not realize that they are all-powerful,
with the result that the catastrophe is delayed and the castle of
Walhalla, insecure but glorious, fronts the storms. Fafnir,
coiled round his hoard, grumbles and grunts; we can hear him
under Europe today; the leaves of the wood already tremble
and the Bird calls its warnings uselessly. Fafnir will destroy us,
but by a blessed dispensation he is stupid and slow, and creation goes on just outside the poisonous blast of his breath.
The Nietzschean would hurry the monster up, the mystic
would say he did not exist, but Wotan, wiser than either,
hastens to create warriors before doom declares itself. The
Valkyries are symbols not only of courage but of intelligence;
they represent the human spirit snatching its opportunity
while the going is good, and one of them even finds time to
love. Brünnhilde's last song hymns the recurrence of love, and
since it is the privilege of art to exaggerate, she goes even
further, and proclaims the love which is eternally triumphant
and feeds upon freedom, and lives.

So that is what I feel about force and violence. It is, alas!
the ultimate reality of this earth, but it does not always get to
the front. Some people call its absences 'decadence'; I call
them 'civilization' and find in such interludes the chief justifi-
cation for the human experiment. I look the other way until
fate strikes me. Whether this is due to courage or to cowardice
in my own case I cannot be sure. But I know that if men had
not looked the other way in the past, nothing of any value
would survive. The people I respect most behave as if they
were immortal and as if society was eternal. Both assumptions
are false: both of them must be accepted as true if we are to go

on eating and working and loving, and are to keep open a few breathing holes for the human spirit. No millennium seems likely to descend upon humanity; no better and stronger League of Nations will be instituted; no form of Christianity and no alternative to Christianity will bring peace to the world or integrity to the individual; no 'change of heart' will occur. And yet we need not despair, indeed, we cannot despair; the evidence of history shows us that men have always insisted on behaving creatively under the shadow of the sword; that they have done their artistic and scientific and domestic stuff for the sake of doing it, and that we had better follow their example under the shadow of the aeroplanes. Others, with more vision or courage than myself, see the salvation of humanity ahead, and will dismiss my conception of civilization as paltry, a sort of tip-and-run game. Certainly it is presumptuous to say that we *cannot* improve, and that Man, who has only been in power for a few thousand years, will never learn to make use of his power. All I mean is that, if people continue to kill one another as they do, the world cannot get better than it is, and that since there are more people than formerly, and their means for destroying one another superior, the world may well get worse. What is good in people – and consequently in the world – is their insistence on creation, their belief in friendship and loyalty for their own sakes; and though Violence remains and is, indeed, the major partner in this muddled establishment, I believe that Creativeness remains too, and will always assume direction when violence sleeps. So, though I am not an optimist, I cannot agree with Sophocles that it were better never to have been born. And although, like Horace, I see no evidence that each batch of births is superior to the last, I leave the field open for the more complacent view. This is such a difficult moment to live in, one cannot help getting gloomy and also a bit rattled, and perhaps short-sighted.

In search of a refuge, we may perhaps turn to hero-worship. But here we shall get no help, in my opinion. Hero-worship is a dangerous vice, and one of the minor merits of a democracy is that it does not encourage it, or produce that unmanageable type of citizen known as the Great Man. It produces instead different kinds of small men – a much finer achievement. But people who cannot get interested in the variety of life, and cannot make up their own minds, get discontented over this, and they long for a hero to bow down before and to follow blindly. It is significant that a hero is an integral part of the authoritarian stock-in-trade today. An efficiency-régime cannot be run without a few heroes stuck about it to carry off the dullness – much as plums have to be put into a bad pudding to make it palatable. One hero at the top and a smaller one each side of him is a favourite arrangement, and the timid and the bored are comforted by the trinity, and, bowing down, feel exalted and strengthened.

No, I distrust Great Men. They produce a desert of uniformity around them and often a pool of blood too, and I always feel a little man's pleasure when they come a cropper. Every now and then one reads in the newspapers some such statement as: 'The *coup d'état* appears to have failed, and Admiral Toma's whereabouts is at present unknown.' Admiral Toma had probably every qualification for being a Great Man – an iron will, personal magnetism, dash, flair, sexlessness – but fate was against him, so he retires to unknown whereabouts instead of parading history with his peers. He fails with a completeness which no artist and no lover can experience, because with them the process of creation is itself an achievement, whereas with him the only possible achievement is success.

I believe in aristocracy, though – if that is the right word, and if a democrat may use it. Not an aristocracy of power, based upon rank and influence, but an aristocracy of the sensitive, the considerate and the plucky. Its members are to be found in all nations and classes, and all through the ages, and there is a secret understanding between them when they meet. They represent the true human tradition, the one permanent victory of our queer race over cruelty and chaos. Thousands of them perish in obscurity, a few are great names. They are sensitive for others as well as for themselves, they are considerate without being fussy, their pluck is not swankiness but the power to endure, and they can take a joke. I give no examples – it is risky to do that – but the reader may as well consider whether this is the type of person he would like to meet and to be, and whether (going farther with me) he would prefer that this type should *not* be an ascetic one. I am against asceticism myself. I am with the old Scotsman who wanted less chastity and more delicacy. I do not feel that my aristocrats are a real aristocracy if they thwart their bodies, since bodies are the instruments through which we register and enjoy the world. Still, I do not insist. This is not a major point. It is clearly possible to be sensitive, considerate and plucky and yet be an ascetic too, and if anyone possesses the first three qualities, I will let him in! On they go – an invincible army, yet not a victorious one. The aristocrats, the elect, the chosen, the Best People – all the words that describe them are false, and all attempts to organize them fail. Again and again Authority, seeing their value, has tried to net them and to utilize them as the Egyptian Priesthood or the Christian Church or the Chinese Civil Service or the Group Movement, or some other worthy stunt. But they slip through the net and are gone; when the door is shut, they are no longer in the room; their temple, as one of them remarked, is the Holiness of the Heart's affection, and their kingdom, though they never possess it, is the wide-open world.

With this type of person knocking about, and constantly crossing one's path if one has eyes to see or hands to feel, the experiment of earthly life cannot be dismissed as a failure. But it may well be hailed as a tragedy, the tragedy being that no device has been found by which these private decencies can be transmitted to public affairs. As soon as people have power they go crooked and sometimes dotty as well, because the possession of power lifts them into a region where normal honesty never pays. For instance, the man who is selling newspapers outside the Houses of Parliament can safely leave his papers to go for a drink and his cap beside them: anyone who takes a paper is sure to drop a copper into the cap. But the men who are inside the Houses of Parliament – they cannot trust one another like that, still less can the Government they compose trust other governments. No caps upon the pavement here, but suspicion, treachery and armaments. The more highly public life is organized the lower does its morality sink; the nations of today behave to each other worse than they ever did in the past, they cheat, rob, bully and bluff, make war without notice, and kill as many women and children as possible; whereas primitive tribes were at all events restrained by taboos. It is a humiliating outlook – though the greater the darkness, the brighter shine the little lights, reassuring one another, signalling: 'Well, at all events, I'm still here. I don't like it very much, but how are you?' Unquenchable lights of my aristocracy! Signals of the invincible army! 'Come along – anyway, let's have a good time while we can.' I think they signal that too.

The Saviour of the future – if ever he comes – will not preach a new Gospel. He will merely utilize my aristocracy, he will make effective the good will and the good temper which are already existing. In other words, he will introduce a new technique. In economics, we are told that if there was a new technique of distribution, there need be no poverty, and people would not starve in one place while crops were being ploughed under in another. A similar change is needed in the sphere of morals and politics. The desire for it is by no means new; it was expressed, for example, in theological terms by Jacopone da Todi over six hundred years ago. 'Ordina questo amore, O tu che m'ami,' he said; 'O thou who lovest me – set this love in order.' His prayer was not granted, and I do not myself believe that it ever will be, but here, and not through a change of heart, is our probable route. Not by becoming better, but by ordering and distributing his native goodness, will Man shut up Force into its box, and so gain time to ex-plore the universe and to set his mark upon it worthily. At present he only explores it at odd moments, when Force is looking the other way, and his divine creativeness appears as a trivial by-product, to be scrapped as soon as the drums beat and the bombers hum.

Such a change, claim the orthodox, can only be made by Christianity, and will be made by it in God's good time: man always has failed and always will fail to organize his own goodness, and it is presumptuous of him to try. This claim – solemn as it is – leaves me cold. I cannot believe that Christianity will ever cope with the present world-wide mess, and I think that such influence as it retains in modern society is due to the money behind it, rather than to its spiritual appeal. It was a spiritual force once, but the indwelling spirit will have to be restated if it is to calm the waters again, and probably restated in a non-Christian form. Naturally a lot of people, and people who are not only good but able and intelligent, will disagree here; they will vehemently deny that Christianity has failed, or they will argue that its failure proceeds from the wickedness of men, and really proves its ultimate success. They have Faith, with a large F. My faith has a very small one, and I only intrude it because these are strenuous and serious days, and one likes to say what one thinks while speech is comparatively free: it may not be free much longer.

The above are the reflections of an individualist and a liberal who has found liberalism crumbling beneath him and at first felt ashamed. Then, looking around, he decided there was no special reason for shame, since other people, whatever they felt, were equally insecure. And as for individualism – there seems no way of getting off this, even if one wanted to. The dictator-hero can grind down his citizens till they are all alike, but he cannot melt them into a single man. That is beyond his power. He can order them to merge, he can incite them to mass-antics, but they are obliged to be born separately, and to die separately, and, owing to these unavoidable termini, will always be running off the totalitarian rails. The memory of birth and the expectation of death always lurk within the human being, making him separate from his fellows and consequently capable of intercourse with them. Naked I came into the world, naked I shall go out of it! And a very good thing too, for it reminds me that I am naked under my shirt, whatever its colour.

1939

STEPHEN LEACOCK (1869–1944)

Oxford As I See It

My private station being that of a university professor, I was
naturally deeply interested in the system of education in England. I was therefore led to make a special visit to Oxford and
to submit the place to a searching scrutiny. Arriving one
afternoon at four o'clock, I stayed at the Mitre Hotel and did
not leave until eleven o'clock next morning. The whole of this
time, except for one hour spent in addressing the undergraduates, was devoted to a close and eager study of the great
university. When I add to this that I had already visited Oxford in 1907 and spent a Sunday at All Souls with Colonel
L. S. Amery, it will be seen at once that my views on Oxford
are based upon observations extending over fourteen years.

At any rate I can at least claim that my acquaintance with
the British university is just as good a basis for reflection and
judgment as that of the numerous English critics who come to
our side of the water. I have known a famous English writer
to arrive at Harvard University in the morning, have lunch
with President Lowell, and then write a whole chapter on the
Excellence of Higher Education in America. I have known
another one come to Harvard, have lunch with President
Lowell and do an entire book on the Decline of Serious Study
in America. Or take the case of my own university. I remember
Mr. Rudyard Kipling coming to McGill and saying in his
address to the undergraduates at 2.30 p.m., 'You have here a
great institution.' But how could he have gathered this infor-

mation? As far as I know he spent the entire morning with Sir Andrew Macphail in his house beside the campus, smoking cigarettes. When I add that he distinctly refused to visit the Palaeontologic Museum, that he saw nothing of our new hydraulic apparatus, or of our classes in Domestic Science, his judgment that we had here a great institution seems a little bit superficial. I can only put beside it, to redeem it in some measure, the hasty and ill-formed judgment expressed by Lord Milner, 'McGill is a noble university': and the rash and indiscreet expression of the Prince of Wales, when we gave him an LL.D. degree, 'McGill has a glorious future.'

To my mind these unthinking judgments about our great college do harm, and I determined, therefore, that anything that I said about Oxford should be the result of the actual observation and real study based upon a bona fide residence in the Mitre Hotel.

On the strength of this basis of experience I am prepared to make the following positive and emphatic statements. Oxford is a noble university. It has a great past. It is at present the greatest university in the world: and it is quite possible that it has a great future. Oxford trains scholars of the real type better than any other place in the world. Its methods are antiquated. It despises science. Its lectures are rotten. It has professors who never teach and students who never learn. It has no order, no arrangement, no system. Its curriculum is unintelligible. It has no president. It has no state legislature to tell it how to teach, and yet – it gets there. Whether we like it or not, Oxford gives something to its students, a life and a mode of thought, which in America as yet we can emulate but not equal.

If anybody doubts this let him go and take a room at the Mitre Hotel (ten and six for a wainscoted bedroom, period of Charles I) and study the place for himself.

These singular results achieved at Oxford are all the more surprising when one considers the distressing conditions under which the students work. The lack of an adequate building fund compels them to go on working in the same old buildings

which they have had for centuries. The buildings at Brasenose
College have not been renewed since the year 1525. In New
College and Magdalen the students are still housed in old
buildings erected in the sixteenth century. At Christ Church I
was shown a kitchen which had been built at the expense of
Cardinal Wolsey in 1527. Incredible though it may seem, they
have no other place to cook in than this and are compelled
to use it today. On the day when I saw this kitchen, four cooks
were busy roasting an ox whole for the students' lunch: this
at least is what I presumed they were doing from the size of
the fireplace used, but it may not have been an ox; perhaps it
was a cow. On a huge table, twelve feet by six and made of
slabs of wood five inches thick, two other cooks were rolling
out a game pie. I estimated it as measuring three feet across.
In this rude way, unchanged since the time of Henry VIII, the
unhappy Oxford students are fed. I could not help contrasting
it with the cosy little boarding houses on Cottage Grove
Avenue where I used to eat when I was a student at Chicago,
or the charming little basement dining-rooms of the students'
boarding houses in Toronto. But then, of course, Henry VIII
never lived in Toronto.

The same lack of a building fund necessitates the Oxford
students living in the identical old boarding houses they had in
the sixteenth and seventeenth centuries. Technically they are
called 'quadrangles', 'closes' and 'rooms'; but I am so broken
in to the usage of my student days that I can't help calling
them boarding houses. In many of these the old stairway has
been worn down by the feet of ten generations of students:
the windows have little latticed panes: there are old names
carved here and there upon the stone, and a thick growth of
ivy covers the walls. The boarding house at St. John's College
dates from 1509, the one at Christ Church from the same
period. A few hundred thousand pounds would suffice to re-
place these old buildings with neat steel and brick structures
like the normal school at Schenectady, N.Y., or the Peel
Street High School at Montreal. But nothing is done. A movement was indeed attempted last autumn towards removing the

ivy from the walls, but the result was unsatisfactory and they are putting it back. Anyone could have told them beforehand that the mere removal of the ivy would not brighten Oxford up, unless at the same time one cleared the stones of the old inscriptions, put in steel fire escapes, and in fact brought the boarding houses up to date.

But Henry VIII being dead, nothing was done. Yet in spite of its dilapidated buildings and its lack of fire escapes, ventilation, sanitation, and up-to-date kitchen facilities, I persist in my assertion that I believe that Oxford, in its way, is the greatest university in the world. I am aware that this is an extreme statement and needs explanation. Oxford is much smaller in numbers, for example, than the State University of Minnesota, and is much poorer. It has, or had till yesterday, fewer students than the University of Toronto. To mention Oxford beside the 26,000 students of Columbia University sounds ridiculous. In point of money, the $39,000,000 endowment of the University of Chicago, and the $43,000,000 of Harvard seem to leave Oxford nowhere. Yet the peculiar thing is that it is not nowhere. By some queer process of its own it seems to get there every time. It was therefore of the very greatest interest to me, as a profound scholar, to try to investigate just how this peculiar excellence of Oxford arises.

It can hardly be due to anything in the curriculum or programme of studies. Indeed, to anyone accustomed to the best models of a university curriculum as it flourishes in the United States and Canada, the programme of studies is frankly quite laughable. There is less Applied Science in the place than would be found with us in a theological college. Hardly a single professor at Oxford would recognize a dynamo if he met it in broad daylight. The Oxford student learns nothing of chemistry, physics, heat, plumbing, electric wiring, gas fitting or the use of a blow torch. Any American college student can run a motor car, take a gasoline engine to pieces, fix a washer on a kitchen tap, mend a broken electric bell, and give an expert opinion on what has gone wrong with the furnace. It is these things indeed which stamp him as a college man, and occasion a very pardonable pride in the minds of his parents. But in all these things the Oxford student is the merest amateur.

This is bad enough. But after all one might say this is only the mechanical side of education. True: but one searches in vain in the Oxford curriculum for any adequate recognition of the higher and more cultured studies. Strange though it seems to us on this side of the Atlantic, there are no courses at Oxford in Housekeeping, or in Salesmanship, or in Advertising, or on Comparative Religion, or on the influence of the Press. There are no lectures whatever on Human Behaviour, on Altruism, on Egotism, or on the Play of Wild Animals. Apparently, the Oxford student does not learn these things. This cuts him off from a great deal of the larger culture of our side of the Atlantic. 'What are you studying this year?' I once asked a fourth-year student at one of our great colleges. 'I am electing Salesmanship and Religion,' he answered. Here was a young man whose training was destined inevitably to turn him into a moral businessman: either that or nothing. At Oxford, Salesmanship is not taught and Religion takes the feeble form of the New Testament. The more one looks at these things the more amazing it becomes that Oxford can produce any results at all.

The effect of the comparison is heightened by the peculiar position occupied at Oxford by the professors' lectures. In the colleges of Canada and the United States the lectures are supposed to be a really necessary and useful part of the students' training. Again and again I have heard the graduates of my own college assert that they had got as much, or nearly as much, out of the lectures at college as out of athletics or the Greek letter society or the Banjo and Mandolin Club. In short, with us the lectures form a real part of the college life. At Oxford it is not so. The lectures, I understand, are given and may even be taken. But they are quite worthless and are not supposed to have anything much to do with the development of the student's mind. 'The lectures here.' said a Canadian student to me, 'are punk.' I appealed to another student to know if this was so. 'I don't know whether I'd call them exactly punk,' he answered, 'but they're certainly rotten.' Other judgments were that the lectures were of no importance: that nobody took them: that they don't matter: that you can take them if you like: that they do you no harm.

It appears further that the professors themselves are not keen on their lectures. If the lectures are called for they give them; if not, the professor's feelings are not hurt. He merely waits and rests his brain until in some later year the students call for his lectures. There are men at Oxford who have rested their brains this way for over thirty years: the accumulated brain power thus dammed up is said to be colossal.

I understand that the key to this mystery is found in the operations of the person called the tutor. It is from him, or rather with him, that the students learn all that they know: one and all are agreed on that. Yet it is a little odd to know just how he does it. 'We go over to his rooms,' said one student, 'and he just lights a pipe and talks to us.' 'We sit round with him,' said another, 'and he simply smokes and goes over our exercises with us.' From this and other evidence I gather that what an Oxford tutor does is to get a little group of students together and smoke at them. Men who have been systematically smoked at for four years turn into ripe scholars. If anybody doubts this, let him go to Oxford and he can see the thing actually in operation. A well-smoked man speaks and writes English with a grace that can be acquired in no other way.

In what was said above, I seem to have been directing criticism against the Oxford professors as such: but I have no intention of doing so. For the Oxford professor and his whole manner of being I have nothing but a profound respect. There is indeed the greatest difference between the modern up-to-date American idea of a professor and the English type. But even with us in older days, in the bygone time when such people as Henry Wadsworth Longfellow were professors, one found the English idea; a professor was supposed to be a venerable kind of person, with snow-white whiskers reaching to his stomach. He was expected to moon about the campus oblivious of the world around him. If you nodded to him he failed to see you. Of money he knew nothing; of business, far less. He was, as his trustees were proud to say of him, 'a child'.

On the other hand he contained within him a reservoir of learning of such depth as to be practically bottomless. None of this learning was supposed to be of any material or commercial benefit to anybody. Its use was in saving the soul and enlarging the mind.

At the head of such a group of professors was one whose beard was even whiter and longer, whose absence of mind was even still greater, and whose knowledge of money, business, and practical affairs was below zero. Him they made the president.

All this is changed in America. A university professor is now a busy, hustling person, approximating as closely to a businessman as he can do it. It is on the businessman that he models himself. He has a little place that he calls his 'office', with a typewriter machine and a stenographer. Here he sits and dictates letters, beginning after the best business models, 'in re yours of the eighth ult., would say, etc., etc.' He writes these letters to students, to his fellow professors, to the president, indeed to any people who will let him write to them. The number of letters that he writes each month is duly counted and set to his credit. If he writes enough he will get a reputation as an 'executive', and big things may happen to him. He may even be asked to step out of the college and take a post as an 'executive' in a soap company or an advertising firm. The man, in short, is a 'hustler', an 'advertiser' whose highest aim is to be a 'live wire'. If he is not, he will presently be dismissed, or, to use the business term, be 'let go', by a board of trustees who are themselves hustlers and live wires. As to the professor's soul, he no longer needs to think of it as it has been handed over along with all the others to a Board of Censors.

The American professor deals with his students according to his lights. It is his business to chase them along over a prescribed ground at a prescribed pace like a flock of sheep. They all go humping together over the hurdles with the pro-

fessor chasing them with a set of 'tests' and 'recitations',
'marks' and 'attendances', the whole apparatus obviously
copied from the time-clock of the businessman's factory. This
process is what is called 'showing results'. The pace set is
necessarily that of the slowest, and thus results in what I have
heard Mr. Edward Beatty describe as the 'convoy system of
education'.

In my own opinion, reached after fifty-two years of profound reflection, this system contains in itself the seeds of
destruction. It puts a premium on dullness and a penalty on
genius. It circumscribes that latitude of mind which is the real
spirit of learning. If we persist in it we shall presently find that
true learning will fly away from our universities and will take
rest wherever some individual and inquiring mind can mark
out its path for itself.

Now the principal reason why I am led to admire Oxford is
that the place is little touched as yet by the measuring of
'results', and by this passion for visible and provable 'efficiency'. The whole system at Oxford is such as to put a
premium on genius and to let mediocrity and dullness go their
way. On the dull student Oxford, after a proper lapse of time,
confers a degree which means nothing more than that he lived
and breathed at Oxford and kept out of jail. This for many
students is as much as society can expect. But for the gifted
student Oxford offers great opportunities. There is no question of his hanging back till the last sheep has jumped over
the fence. He need wait for no one. He may move forward as
fast as he likes, following the bent of his genius. If he has in
him any ability beyond that of the common herd, his tutor,
interested in his studies, will smoke at him until he kindles
him into a flame. For the tutor's soul is not harassed by herd-
ing dull students, with dismissal hanging by a thread over his
head in the classroom. The American professor has no time
to be interested in a clever student. He has time to be interested
in his 'deportment', his letter writing, his executive work, and
his organizing ability and his hope of promotion to a soap
factory. But with that his mind is exhausted. The student of

genius merely means to him a student who gives no trouble, who passes all his 'tests', and is present at all his 'recitations'. Such a student also, if he can be trained to be a hustler and an advertiser, will undoubtedly 'make good'. But beyond that the professor does not think of him. The everlasting principle of equality has inserted itself in a place where it has no right to be, and where inequality is the breath of life.

American or Canadian college trustees would be horrified at the notion of professors who apparently do no work, give few or no lectures and draw their pay merely for existing. Yet these are really the only kind of professors worth having – I mean, men who can be trusted with a vague general mission in life, with a salary guaranteed at least till their death, and a sphere of duties entrusted solely to their own consciences and the promptings of their own desires. Such men are rare, but a single one of them, when found, is worth ten 'executives' and a dozen 'organizers'.

The excellence of Oxford, then, as I see it, lies in the peculiar vagueness of the organization of its work. It starts from the assumption that the professor is a really learned man whose sole interest lies in his own sphere: and that a student, or at least the only student with whom the university cares to reckon seriously, is a young man who desires to know. This is an ancient mediaeval attitude long since buried in more up-to-date places under successive strata of compulsory education, state teaching, the democratization of knowledge, and the substitution of the shadow for the substance and the casket for the gem. No doubt, in newer places the thing has got to be so. Higher education in America flourishes chiefly as a qualification for entrance into a money-making profession, and not as a thing in itself. But in Oxford one can still see the surviving outline of a nobler type of structure and a higher inspiration.

I do not mean to say, however, that my judgment of Oxford is one undiluted stream of praise. In one respect at least I think that Oxford has fallen away from the high ideals of the Middle Ages. I refer to the fact that it admits women students to its studies. In the Middle Ages women were regarded with a peculiar chivalry long since lost. It was taken for granted that their brains were too delicately poised to allow them to learn anything. It was presumed that their minds were so exquisitely hung that intellectual effort might disturb them. The present age has gone to the other extreme: and this is seen nowhere more than in the crowding of women into colleges originally designed for men. Oxford, I regret to find, has not stood out against this change.

To a profound scholar like myself, the presence of these young women, many of them most attractive, flittering up and down the streets of Oxford in their caps and gowns, is very distressing.

Who is to blame for this and how they first got in I do not know. But I understand that they first of all built a private college of their own close to Oxford, and then edged themselves in foot by foot. If this is so they only followed up the precedent of the recognized method in use in America. When an American college is established, the women go and build a college of their own overlooking the grounds. Then they put on becoming caps and gowns and stand and look over the fence at the college athletics. The male undergraduates, who were originally and by nature a hardy lot, were not easily disturbed. But inevitably some of the senior trustees fell in love with the first year girls and became convinced that coeducation was a noble cause. American statistics show that between 1880 and 1900 the number of trustees and senior professors who married girl undergraduates or who wanted to do so reached a percentage of – I forget the exact percentage; it was either a hundred or a little over.

I don't know just what happened at Oxford but presumably something of the sort took place. In any case the women are now all over the place. They attend the college lectures, they row in a boat, and they perambulate the High Street. They are even offering a serious competition against the men. Last year they carried off the ping-pong championship and took the chancellor's prize for needlework, while in music, cooking and millinery the men are said to be nowhere.

There is no doubt that unless Oxford puts the women out while there is yet time, they will overrun the whole university. What this means to the progress of learning few can tell and those who know are afraid to say.

Cambridge University, I am glad to see, still sets its face sternly against this innovation. I am reluctant to count any superiority in the University of Cambridge. Having twice visited Oxford, having made the place a subject of profound study for many hours at a time, having twice addressed its undergraduates, and having stayed at the Mitre Hotel, I consider myself an Oxford man. But I must admit that Cambridge has chosen the wiser part.

Last autumn, while I was in London on my voyage of discovery, a vote was taken at Cambridge to see if the women who have already a private college nearby should be admitted to the university. They were triumphantly shut out; and as a fit and proper sign of enthusiasm the undergraduates went over in a body and knocked down the gates of the women's college. I know that it is a terrible thing to say that anyone approved of this. All the London papers came out with headings that read – ARE OUR UNDERGRADUATES TURNING INTO BABOONS? and so on. The *Manchester Guardian* draped its pages in black and even the London *Morning Post* was afraid to take bold ground in the matter. But I do know also that there was a great deal of secret chuckling and jubilation in the London clubs. Nothing was expressed openly. The men of England have been too terrorized by the women for that. But in safe corners of the club, out of earshot of the waiters and away from casual strangers, little groups of elderly men chuckled quietly together. 'Knocked down their gates, eh?' said the wicked old men to one another, and then whispered guiltily behind an uplifted hand, 'Serve 'em right.' Nobody dared to say anything outside. If they had someone would have got up and asked a question in the House of Commons. When this is done all England falls flat upon its face.

But for my part when I heard of the Cambridge vote, I felt

as Lord Chatham did when he said in Parliament, 'Sir, I re-
joice that America has resisted.' For I have long harboured
views of my own upon the higher education of women. In
these days, however, it requires no little hardihood to utter a
single word of criticism against it. It is like throwing half a
brick through the glass roof of a conservatory. It is bound to
make trouble. Let me hasten, therefore, to say that I believe
most heartily in the higher education of women; in fact, the
higher the better. The only question to my mind is: What is
'higher education' and how do you get it? With which goes
the secondary inquiry, What is a woman and is she just the
same as a man? I know that it sounds a terrible thing to say in
these days, but I don't believe she is.

Let me say also that when I speak of coeducation I speak
of what I know. I was coeducated myself some thirty-five
years ago, at the very beginning of the thing. I learned my
Greek alongside of a bevy of beauty on the opposite benches
that mashed up the irregular verbs for us very badly. Incidentally, those girls are all married long since, and all the
Greek they know now you could put under a thimble. But of
that presently.

I have had further experience as well. I spent three years in
the graduate school of Chicago, where coeducational girls
were as thick as autumn leaves – and some thicker. And as a
college professor at McGill University in Montreal, I have
taught mingled classes of men and women for twenty years.

On the basis of which experience I say with assurance that
the thing is a mistake and has nothing to recommend it but its
relative cheapness. Let me emphasize this last point and have
done with it. Coeducation is of course a great economy. To
teach ten men and ten women in a single class of twenty costs
only half as much as to teach two classes. Where economy
must rule, then, the thing has got to be. But where the discussion turns not on what is cheapest, but on what is best, then
the case is entirely different.

The fundamental trouble is that men and women are different creatures, with different minds and different aptitudes and

different paths in life. There is no need to raise here the question of which is superior and which is inferior (though I think, the Lord help me, I know the answer to that too). The point lies in the fact that they are different.

But the mad passion for equality has masked this obvious fact. When women began to demand, quite rightly, a share in higher education, they took for granted that they wanted the same curriculum as the men. They never stopped to ask whether their aptitudes were not in various directions higher and better than those of the men, and whether it might not be better for their sex to cultivate the things which were best suited to their minds. Let me be more explicit. In all that goes with physical and mathematical science, women, on the average, are far below the standard of men. There are, of course, exceptions. But they prove nothing. It is no use to quote to me the case of some brilliant girl who stood first in physics at Cornell. That's nothing. There is an elephant in the zoo that can count up to ten, yet I refuse to reckon myself his inferior.

Tabulated results spread over years, and the actual experience of those who teach show that in the whole domain of mathematics and physics women are outclassed. At McGill the girls of our first year have wept over their failures in elementary physics these twenty-five years. It is time that someone dried their tears and took away the subject.

But, in any case, examination tests are never the whole story. To those who know, a written examination is far from being a true criterion of capacity. It demands too much of mere memory, imitativeness, and the insidious willingness to absorb other people's ideas. Parrots and crows would do admirably in examinations. Indeed, the colleges are full of them.

But take, on the other hand, all that goes with the aesthetic side of education, with imaginative literature and the cult of beauty. Here women are, or at least ought to be, the superiors of men. Women were in primitive times the first story-tellers. They are still so at the cradle-side. The original college woman was the witch, with her incantations and her prophecies and the glow of her bright imagination, and if brutal men of duller brains had not burned it out of her, she would be incanting still. To my thinking, we need more witches in the colleges and less physics.

I have seen such young witches myself – if I may keep the word: I like it – in colleges such as Wellesley in Massachusetts and Bryn Mawr in Pennsylvania, where there isn't a man allowed within the three-mile limit. To my mind, they do infinitely better thus by themselves. They are freer, less restrained. They discuss things openly in their classes; they lift up their voices, and they speak, whereas a girl in such a place as McGill, with men all about her, sits for four years as silent as a frog full of shot.

But there is a deeper trouble still. The careers of the men and women who go to college together are necessarily different, and the preparation is all aimed at the man's career. The men are going to be lawyers, doctors, engineers, businessmen, and politicians. And the women are not.

There is no use pretending about it. It may sound an awful thing to say, but the women are going to be married. That is, and always has been, their career; and, what is more, they know it; and even at college, while they are studying algebra and political economy, they have their eye on it sideways all the time. The plain fact is that, after a girl has spent four years of her time and a great deal of her parents' money in equipping herself for a career that she is never going to have, the wretched creature goes and gets married, and in a few years she has forgotten which is the hypotenuse of a right-angled triangle, and she doesn't care. She has much better things to think of.

At this point someone will shriek: 'But surely, even for marriage, isn't it right that a girl should have a college education?' To which I hasten to answer: most assuredly. I freely admit that a girl who knows algebra, or once knew it, is a far more charming companion and a nobler wife and mother than a girl who doesn't know x from y. But the point is this: Does the higher education that fits a man to be a lawyer also fit a person to be a wife and mother? Or, in other words, is a lawyer a wife and mother? I say he is not. Granted that a girl is to spend four years in time and four thousand dollars in money in going to college, why train her for a career that she is never going to adopt? Why not give her an education that will have a meaning and a harmony with the real life that she is to follow?

For example, suppose that during her four years every girl lucky enough to get a higher education spent at least six months of it in the training and discipline of a hospital as a nurse. There is more education and character-making in that than in a whole bucketful of algebra.

But no, the woman insists on snatching her share of an education designed by Erasmus or William of Wykeham or William of Occam for the creation of scholars and lawyers; and when later on in her home there is a sudden sickness or accident, and the life or death of those nearest to her hangs upon skill and knowledge and a trained fortitude in emergency, she must needs send in all haste for a hired woman to fill the place that she herself has never learned to occupy.

But I am not here trying to elaborate a whole curriculum. I am only trying to indicate that higher education for the man is one thing, for the woman another. Nor do I deny the fact that women have got to earn their living. Their higher education must enable them to do that. They cannot all marry on their graduation day. But that is no great matter. No scheme of education that anyone is likely to devise will fail in this respect.

The positions that they hold as teachers or civil servants they would fill better if their education were fitted to their wants.

Some few, a small minority, really and truly 'have a career' – husbandless and childless – in which the sacrifice is great and the honour to them, perhaps, all the higher. And others no doubt dream of a career in which a husband and a group of blossoming children are carried as an appendage to a busy life at the bar or on the platform. But all such are the mere minority, so small as to make no difference to the general argument.

But there – I have written quite enough to make plenty of trouble except perhaps at Cambridge University. So I turn with relief to my general study of Oxford. Viewing the situation as a whole, I am led then to the conclusion that there must be something in the life of Oxford itself that makes for higher learning. Smoked at by his tutor, fed in Henry VIII's kitchen, and sleeping in a tangle of ivy, the student evidently gets something not easily obtained in America. And the more I reflect on the matter the more I am convinced that it is the sleeping in the ivy that does it. How different it is from student life as I remember it!

When I was a student at the University of Toronto thirty years ago, I lived – from start to finish – in seventeen different boarding houses. As far as I am aware these houses have not, or not yet, been marked with tablets. But they are still to be found in the vicinity of McCaul and D'Arcy and St. Patrick streets. Anyone who doubts the truth of what I have to say may go and look at them.

I was not alone in the nomadic life that I led. There were hundreds of us drifting about in this fashion from one melancholy habitation to another. We lived as a rule two or three in a house, sometimes alone. We dined in the basement. We always had beef, done up in some way after it was dead, and there were always soda biscuits on the table. They used to have a brand of soda biscuits in those days in the Toronto boarding houses that I have not seen since. They were better than dog biscuits but with not so much snap. My contemporaries will all remember them. A great many of the leading barristers and professional men of Toronto were fed on them.

In the life we led we had practically no opportunities for association on a large scale, no common rooms, no reading rooms, nothing. We never saw the magazines – personally I didn't even know the names of them. The only interchange of ideas we ever got was by going over to the Caer Howell Hotel on University Avenue and interchanging them there.

I mention these melancholy details not for their own sake but merely to emphasize the point that when I speak of students' dormitories, and the larger life which they offer, I speak of what I know.

If we had had at Toronto, when I was a student, the kind of dormitories and dormitory life that they have at Oxford, I don't think I would ever have graduated. I'd have been there still. The trouble is that the universities on our continent are only just waking up to the idea of what a university should mean. They were, very largely, instituted and organized with the idea that a university was a place where young men were sent to absorb the contents of books and to listen to lectures in the class rooms. The student was pictured as a pallid creature, burning what was called the 'midnight oil', his wan face bent over his desk. If you wanted to do something for him you gave him a book: if you wanted to do something really large on his behalf you gave him a whole basketful of them. If you wanted to go still further and be a benefactor to the college at large, you endowed a competitive scholarship and set two or more pallid students working themselves to death to get it.

The real thing for the student is the life and environment that surrounds him. All that he really learns he learns, in a sense, by the active operation of his own intellect and not as the passive recipient of lectures. And for this active operation what he really needs most is the continued and intimate contact with his fellows. Students must live together and eat together, talk and smoke together. Experience shows that that is how their minds really grow. And they must live together in a rational and comfortable way. They must eat in a big dining room or hall, with oak beams across the ceiling, and the stained glass in the windows, and with a shield or tablet here or there upon the wall, to remind them between times of the men who went before them and left a name worthy of the memory of the college. If a student is to get from his college what it ought to give him, a college dormitory, with the life in common that it brings, is his absolute right. A university that fails to give it to him is cheating him.

If I were founding a university – and I say it with all the seriousness of which I am capable – I would found first a smoking room; then when I had a little more money in hand I would found a dormitory; then after that, or more probably with it, a decent reading room and a library. After that, if I still had money over that I couldn't use, I would hire a professor and get some textbooks.

This chapter has sounded in the most part like a continuous eulogy of Oxford with but little in favour of our American colleges. I turn therefore with pleasure to the more congenial task of showing what is wrong with Oxford and with the English university system generally, and the aspect in which our American universities far excel the British.

The point is that Henry VIII is dead. The English are so proud of what Henry VIII and the benefactors of earlier centuries did for the universities that they forget the present. There is little or nothing in England to compare with the magnificent generosity of individuals, provinces, and states, which is building up the colleges of the United States and Canada. There used to be. But by some strange confusion of thought the English people admire the noble gifts of Cardinal Wolsey and Henry VIII and Queen Margaret, and do not realize that the Carnegies and Rockefellers and the William Macdonalds are the Cardinal Wolseys of today. The University of Chicago was founded upon oil. McGill University rests largely on a basis of tobacco. In America the world of commerce and business levies on itself a noble tribute in favour of the higher learning. In England, with a few conspicuous exceptions, such as that at Bristol, there is little of the sort. The feudal families are content with what their remote ancestors have done: they do not try to emulate it in any great degree.

In the long run this must count. Of all the various reforms that are talked of at Oxford, and of all the imitations of American methods that are suggested, the only one worth while, to my thinking, is to capture a few millionaires, give them honorary degrees at a million pounds sterling apiece, and tell them to imagine that they are Henry VIII. I give Oxford warning that if this is not done the place will not last another two centuries.

1922

[handwritten annotations: Cerulean — dahabieh — large sailing boat used by travellers on... / morbid — of the nature or indicative of disease / bemoan / octavo — each page is 1/8 of one piece of paper / filially / Biskra]

MAX BEERBOHM (1872–1956)

[handwritten: biograph? upstart — claims more imgt. / links — continuity / — dream?]

The Crime

[handwritten: appr. of title? / — expectations?]

[handwritten: Why no commas?]

On a bleak wet stormy afternoon at the outset of last year's Spring, I was in a cottage, all alone, and knowing that I must be all alone till evening. It was a remote cottage, in a remote county, and had been 'let furnished' by its owner. My spirits are easily affected by weather, and I hate solitude. And I dislike to be master of things that are not mine. 'Be careful not to break us,' say the glass and china. 'You'd better not spill ink on *me*,' growls the carpet. 'None of your dog's-earing, thumb-marking, back-breaking tricks *here*!' snarl the books.

[handwritten: fund of (I) / — setting / — person / situation / Effect]

The books in this cottage looked particularly disagreeable – horrid little upstarts of this and that scarlet or cerulean 'series' of 'standard' authors. Having gloomily surveyed them, I turned my back on them, and watched the rain streaming down the latticed window, whose panes seemed likely to be shattered at any moment by the wind. I have known men who constantly visit the Central Criminal Court, visit also the scenes where famous crimes were committed, form their own theories of those crimes, collect souvenirs of those crimes, and call themselves Criminologists. As for me, my interest in crime is, alas, merely morbid. I did not know, as those others would doubtless have known, that the situation in which I found myself was precisely of the kind most conducive to the darkest deeds. I did but bemoan it, and think of Lear in the hovel on the heath. The wind howled in the chimney, and the rain had begun to sputter right down it, so that the fire was

[handwritten: TRANS? / Ink / effect para... of m... / Lear — The wind howled]

beginning to hiss in a very sinister manner. Suppose the fire went out! It looked as if it meant to. I snatched the pair of bellows that hung beside it. I plied them vigorously. 'Now mind! – not *too* vigorously. We aren't yours!' they wheezed. I handled them more gently. But I did not release them till they had secured me a steady blaze.

I sat down before that blaze. Despair had been warded off. Gloom, however, remained; and gloom grew. I felt that I should prefer any one's thoughts to mine. I rose, I returned to the books. A dozen or so of those which were on the lowest of the three shelves were full-sized, were octavo, looked as though they had been bought to be read. I would exercise my undoubted right to read one of them. Which of them? I gradually decided on a novel by a well-known writer whose works, though I had several times had the honour of meeting her, were known to me only by repute.

I knew nothing of them that was not good. The lady's 'output' had not been at all huge, and it was agreed that her 'level' was high. I had always gathered that the chief characteristic of her work was its great 'vitality'. The book in my hand was a third edition of her latest novel, and at the end of it were numerous press-notices, at which I glanced for confirmation. 'Immense vitality', yes, said one critic. 'Full', said another, 'of an intense vitality.' 'A book that will live,' said a third. How on earth did he know that? I was, however, very willing to believe in the vitality of this writer for all present purposes. Vitality was a thing in which she herself, her talk, her glance, her gestures, abounded. She and they had been, I remembered, rather too much for me. The first time I met her, she said something that I lightly and mildly disputed. On no future occasion did I stem any opinion of hers. Not that she had been rude. Far from it. She had but in a sisterly, brotherly way, and yet in a way that was filially eager too, asked me to explain my point. I did my best. She was all attention. But I was conscious that my best, under her eye, was not good. She was quick to help me: she said for me just what I had tried to say, and proceeded to show me just why it was wrong. I smiled the gallant smile of a man who regards women as all the more adorable because logic is *not* their strong point, bless them! She asked – not aggressively, but strenuously, as one who dearly loves a joke – what I was smiling at. Altogether, a chastening encounter; and my memory of it was tinged with a feeble resentment. How she had scored. No man likes to be worsted in argument by a woman. And I fancy that to be vanquished by a feminine writer is the kind of defeat least of all agreeable to a man who writes. A 'sex war', we are often told, is to be one of the features of the world's future – women demanding the right to do men's work, and men refusing, resisting, counter-attacking. It seems likely enough. One can believe anything of the world's future. Yet one conceives that not all men, if this particular evil come to pass, will stand packed shoulder to shoulder against all women. One does not feel that the dockers will be very bitter against such women as want to be miners, or the plumbers frown much upon the would-be steeple-jills. I myself have never had my sense of fitness jarred, nor a spark of animosity roused in me, by a woman practising any of the fine arts – except the art of writing. That she should write a few little poems or *pensées*, or some impressions of a trip in a dahabieh as far as (say) Biskra, or even a short story or two, seems to me not wholly amiss, even though she do such things for publication. But that she should be an habitual, professional author, with a passion for her art, and a fountain-pen and an agent, and sums down in advance of royalties on sales in Canada and Australia, and a profound knowledge of human character, and an essentially sane outlook, is somehow incongruous with my notions – my mistaken notions, if you will – of what she ought to be.

'Has a profound knowledge of human character, and an essentially sane outlook,' said one of the critics quoted at the end of the book that I had chosen. The wind and the rain in the chimney had not abated, but the fire was bearing up bravely. So would I. I would read cheerfully and without prejudice. I poked the fire and, pushing my chair slightly back, lest the heat should warp the book's covers, began

Chapter I. A woman sat writing in a summer-house at the end of a small garden that overlooked a great valley in Surrey. The description of her was calculated to make her very admirable – a thorough *woman*, not strictly beautiful, but likely to be thought beautiful by those who knew her well; not dressed as though she gave much heed to her clothes, but dressed in a fashion that exactly harmonized with her special type. Her pen 'travelled' rapidly across the foolscap, and while it did so she was described in more and more detail. But at length she came to a 'knotty point' in what she was writing. She paused, she pushed back the hair from her temples, she looked forth at the valley; and now the landscape was described, but not at all exhaustively, it, for the writer soon overcame her difficulty, and her pen travelled faster than ever, till suddenly there was a cry of 'Mammy!' and in rushed a seven-year-old child, in conjunction with whom she was more than ever admirable; after which the narrative skipped back across eight years, and the woman became a girl giving as yet no token of future eminence in literature, but – I had an impulse which I obeyed almost before I was conscious of it.

Nobody could have been more surprised than I was at what I had done – done so neatly, so quietly and gently. The book stood closed, upright, with its back to me, just as on a book-shelf, behind the bars of the grate. There it was. And it gave forth, as the flames crept up the blue cloth sides of it, a pleasant though acrid smell. My astonishment had passed, giving place to an exquisite satisfaction. How pottering and fumbling a thing was even the best kind of written criticism! I understood the contempt felt by the man of action for the man of words. But what pleased me most was that at last, actually, I, at my age, I of all people, had committed a crime – was guilty of a crime. I had power to revoke it. I might write to my bookseller for an unburnt copy, and place it on the shelf where this one had stood – this gloriously glowing one. I would do nothing of the sort. What I had done I had done. I would wear forever on my conscience the white rose of theft and the red rose of arson. If hereafter the owner of this cottage happened to miss that volume – let him! If he were fool enough to write to me about it, would I share my grand secret with him? No. Gently, with his poker, I prodded that volume further among the coals. The all-but-consumed binding shot forth little tongues of bright colour – flamelets of sapphire, amethyst, emerald. Charming! Could even the author herself not admire them? Perhaps. Poor woman! – I had scored now, scored so perfectly that I felt myself to be almost a brute while I poked off the loosened black outer pages and led the fire on to pages that were but pale brown.

These were quickly devoured. But it seemed to me that whenever I left the fire to forage for itself it made little headway. I pushed the book over on its side. The flames closed on it, but presently, licking their lips, fell back, as though they had had enough. I took the tongs and put the book upright again, and raked it fore and aft. It seemed almost as thick as ever. With poker and tongs I carved it into two, three sections – the inner pages flashing white as when they were sent to the binders. Strange! Aforetime, a book was burnt now and again in the market-place by the common hangman. Was he, I wondered, paid by the hour? I had always supposed the thing quite easy for him – a bright little, brisk little conflagration, and so home. Perhaps other books were less resistant than this one? I began to feel that the critics were more right than they knew. Here was a book that had indeed an intense vitality, and an immense vitality. It was a book that would live – do what one might. I vowed it should not. I subdivided it, spread it, redistributed it. Ever and anon my eye would be caught by some sentence or fragment of a sentence in the midst of a charred page before the flames crept over it, 'lways loathed you, bu', I remember; and 'ning. Tolstoi was right.' Who had always loathed whom? And what, what, had Tolstoi been right about? I had an absurd but genuine desire to know. Too late! Confound the woman! – she was scoring again. I furiously drove her pages into the yawning crimson jaws of the coals. Those jaws had lately been golden. Soon, to my horror, they seemed to be growing grey. They seemed to be closing – on nothing. Flakes of black paper, full-sized layers of paper brown and white, began to hide them from me altogether. I sprinkled a boxful of wax matches. I resumed the bellows. I lunged with the poker. I held a newspaper over the whole grate. I did all that inspiration could suggest, or skill accomplish. Vainly. The fire went out – darkly, dismally, gradually, quite out.

How she had scored again! But she did not know it. I felt no bitterness against her as I lay back in my chair, inert, listening to the storm that was still raging. I blamed only myself. I had done wrong. The small room became very cold. Whose fault was that but my own? I had done wrong hastily, but had done it and been glad of it. I had not remembered the words a wise king wrote long ago, that the lamp of the wicked shall be put out, and that the way of transgressors is hard.

1920

Woman Scored 1)
              2)
              3)

Scoring
Vitality
Series — Repetition 3
Irony < Suspense

Crime
Violence

VIRGINIA WOOLF (1882–1941)

How Should One Read a Book?

In the first place, I want to emphasize the note of interrogation at the end of my title. Even if I could answer the question for myself, the answer would apply only to me and not to you. The only advice, indeed, that one person can give another about reading is to take no advice, to follow your own instincts, to use your own reason, to come to your own conclusions. If this is agreed between us, then I feel at liberty to put forward a few ideas and suggestions because you will not allow them to fetter that independence which is the most important quality that a reader can possess. After all, what laws can be laid down about books? The battle of Waterloo was certainly fought on a certain day; but is *Hamlet* a better play than *Lear*? Nobody can say. Each must decide that question for himself. To admit authorities, however heavily furred and gowned, into our libraries and let them tell us how to read, what to read, what value to place upon what we read, is to destroy the spirit of freedom which is the breath of those sanctuaries. Everywhere else we may be bound by laws and conventions – there we have none.

But to enjoy freedom, if the platitude is pardonable, we have of course to control ourselves. We must not squander our powers, helplessly and ignorantly, squirting half the house in order to water a single rose-bush; we must train them, exactly and powerfully, here on the very spot. This, it may be, is one of the first difficulties that faces us in a library. What is 'the very spot'? There may well seem to be nothing but a conglomeration and huddle of confusion. Poems and novels, histories and memoirs, dictionaries and blue-books; books written in all languages by men and women of all tempers, races, and ages jostle each other on the shelf. And outside the donkey brays, the women gossip at the pump, the colts gallop across the fields. Where are we to begin? How are we to bring order into this multitudinous chaos and so get the deepest and widest pleasure from what we read?

It is simple enough to say that since books have classes – fiction, biography, poetry – we should separate them and take from each what it is right that each should give us. Yet few people ask from books what books can give us. Most commonly we come to books with blurred and divided minds, asking of fiction that it shall be true, of poetry that it shall be false, of biography that it shall be flattering, of history that it shall enforce our own prejudices. If we could banish all such preconceptions when we read, that would be an admirable beginning. Do not dictate to your author; try to become him. Be his fellow-worker and accomplice. If you hang back, and reserve and criticize at first, you are preventing yourself from getting the fullest possible value from what you read. But if you open your mind as widely as possible, then signs and hints of almost imperceptible fineness, from the twist and turn of the first sentences, will bring you into the presence of a human being unlike any other. Steep yourself in this, acquaint yourself with this, and soon you will find that your author is giving you, or attempting to give you, something far more definite. The thirty-two chapters of a novel – if we consider how to read a novel first – are an attempt to make something as formed and controlled as a building: but words are more impalpable than bricks; reading is a longer and more complicated process than seeing. Perhaps the quickest way to understand the elements of what a novelist is doing is not to read, but to write; to make your own experiment with the dangers and difficulties of words. Recall, then, some event that has left a distinct impression on you – how at the corner

of the street, perhaps, you passed two people talking. A tree
shook; an electric light danced; the tone of the talk was
comic, but also tragic; a whole vision, an entire conception,
seemed contained in that moment.

But when you attempt to reconstruct it in words, you will
find that it breaks into a thousand conflicting impressions.
Some must be subdued; others emphasized; in the process
you will lose, probably, all grasp upon the emotion itself.
Then turn from your blurred and littered pages to the opening
pages of some great novelist – Defoe, Jane Austen, Hardy.
Now you will be better able to appreciate their mastery. It is
not merely that we are in the presence of a different person –
Defoe, Jane Austen, or Thomas Hardy – but that we are
living in a different world. Here, in *Robinson Crusoe*, we are
trudging a plain high road; one thing happens after another;
the fact and the order of the fact is enough. But if the open
air and adventure mean everything to Defoe they mean nothing to Jane Austen. Hers is the drawing-room, and people
talking, and by the many mirrors of their talk revealing their
characters. And if, when we have accustomed ourselves to the
drawing-room and its reflections, we turn to Hardy, we are
once more spun round. The moors are round us and the stars
are above our heads. The other side of the mind is now exposed – the dark side that comes uppermost in solitude, not
the light side that shows in company. Our relations are not
towards people, but towards Nature and destiny. Yet different
as these worlds are, each is consistent with itself. The maker of
each is careful to observe the laws of his own perspective, and
however great a strain they may put upon us they will never
confuse us, as lesser writers so frequently do, by introducing
two different kinds of reality into the same book. Thus to go
from one great novelist to another – from Jane Austen to
Hardy, from Peacock to Trollope, from Scott to Meredith – is
to be wrenched and uprooted; to be thrown this way and then
that. To read a novel is a difficult and complex art. You must
be capable not only of great fineness of perception, but of
great boldness of imagination if you are going to make use of

all that the novelist – the great artist – gives you.

But a glance at the heterogeneous company on the shelf will show you that writers are very seldom 'great artists'; far more often a book makes no claim to be a work of art at all. These biographies and autobiographies, for example, lives of great men, of men long dead and forgotten, that stand cheek by jowl with the novels and poems, are we to refuse to read them because they are not 'art'? Or shall we read them, but read them in a different way, with a different aim? Shall we read them in the first place to satisfy that curiosity which possesses us sometimes when in the evening we linger in front of a house where the lights are lit and the blinds not yet drawn, and each floor of the house shows us a different section of human life in being? Then we are consumed with curiosity about the lives of these people – the servants gossiping, the gentlemen dining, the girl dressing for a party, the old woman at the window with her knitting. Who are they, what are they, what are their names, their occupations, their thoughts, and adventures?

Biographies and memoirs answer such questions, light up innumerable such houses; they show us people going about their daily affairs, toiling, failing, succeeding, eating, hating, loving, until they die. And sometimes as we watch, the house fades and the iron railings vanish and we are out at sea; we are hunting, sailing, fighting; we are among savages and soldiers; we are taking part in great campaigns. Or if we like to stay here in England, in London, still the scene changes; the street narrows; the house becomes small, cramped, diamond-paned, and malodorous. We see a poet, Donne, driven from such a house because the walls were so thin that when the children cried their voices cut through them. We can follow him, through the paths that lie in the pages of books, to Twickenham; to Lady Bedford's Park, a famous meeting-ground for nobles and poets; and then turn our steps to Wilton, the great house under the downs, and hear Sidney read the *Arcadia* to his sister; and ramble among the very marshes and see the very herons that figure in that famous romance; and then again travel north with that other Lady Pembroke, Anne Clifford, to her wild moors, or plunge into the city and control our merriment at the sight of Gabriel Harvey in his black velvet suit arguing about poetry with Spenser. Nothing is more fascinating than to grope and stumble in the alternate darkness and splendour of Elizabethan London. But there is no staying there. The Temples and the Swifts, the Harleys and the St. Johns beckon us on; hour upon hour can be spent disentangling their quarrels and deciphering their characters; and when we tire of them we can stroll on, past a lady in black wearing diamonds, to Samuel Johnson and Goldsmith and Garrick; or cross the Channel, if we like, and meet Voltaire and Diderot, Madame du Deffand; and so back to England and Twickenham – how certain places repeat themselves and certain names! – where Lady Bedford had her Park once and Pope lived later, to Walpole's home at Strawberry Hill. But Walpole introduces us to such a swarm of new acquaintances, there are so many houses to visit and bells to ring that we may well hesitate for a moment on the Miss Berrys' doorstep, for example, when behold, up comes Thackeray; he is the friend of the woman whom Walpole loved; so that merely by going from friend to friend, from garden to garden, from house to house, we have passed from one end of English literature to another and wake to find ourselves here again in the present, if we can so differentiate this moment from all that have gone before. This, then, is one of the ways in which we can read these lives and letters; we can make them light up the many windows of the past; we can watch the famous dead in their familiar habits and fancy sometimes that we are very close and can surprise their secrets, and sometimes we may pull out a play or a poem that they have written and see whether it reads differently in the presence of the author. But this again rouses other questions. How far, we must ask ourselves, is a book influenced by its writer's life – how far is it safe to let the man interpret the writer? How far shall we resist or give way to the sympathies and antipathies that the man himself arouses in us – so sensitive are words, so receptive of the character of the author? These are questions that press upon us when we read lives and letters, and we must answer them for ourselves, for nothing can be more fatal than to be guided by the preferences of others in a matter so personal.

But also we can read such books with another aim, not to throw light on literature, not to become familiar with famous people, but to refresh and exercise our own creative powers. Is there not an open window on the right hand of the bookcase? How delightful to stop reading and look out! How stimulating the scene is, in its unconsciousness, its irrelevance, its perpetual movement – the colts galloping around the field, the woman filling her pail at the well, the donkey throwing back his head and emitting his long, acrid moan. The greater part of any library is nothing but the record of such fleeting moments in the lives of men, women, and donkeys. Every literature, as it grows old, has its rubbish-heap, its record of vanished moments and forgotten lives told in faltering and feeble accents that have perished. But if you give yourself up to the delight of rubbish-reading you will be surprised, indeed you will be overcome, by the relics of human life that have been cast out to moulder. It may be one letter – but what a vision it gives! It may be a few sentences – but what vistas they suggest! Sometimes a whole story will come together with such beautiful humour and pathos and completeness that it seems as if a great novelist had been at work, yet it is only an old actor, Tate Wilkinson, remembering the strange story of Captain Jones; it is only a young subaltern serving under Arthur Wellesley and falling in love with a pretty girl at Lisbon; it is only Maria Allen letting fall her sewing in the empty drawing-room and sighing how she wishes she had taken Dr. Burney's good advice and had never eloped with her Rishy. None of this has any value; it is negligible in the extreme; yet how absorbing it is now and again to go through the rubbish-heaps and find rings and scissors and broken noses buried in the huge past and try to piece them together while the colt gallops round the field, the woman fills her pail at the well, and the donkey brays.

But we tire of rubbish-reading in the long run. We tire of searching for what is needed to complete the half-truth which is all that the Wilkinsons, the Bunburys, and the Maria Allens are able to offer us. They had not the artist's power of mastering and eliminating; they could not tell the whole truth even about their own lives; they have disfigured the story that might have been so shapely. Facts are all that they can offer us, and facts are a very inferior form of fiction. Thus the desire grows upon us to have done with half-statements and approximations; to cease from searching out the minute shades of human character, to enjoy the greater abstractness, the purer truth of fiction. Thus we create the mood, intense and generalized, unaware of detail, but stressed by some regular, recurrent beat, whose natural expression is poetry; and that is the time to read poetry when we are almost able to write it.

> *Western wind, when wilt thou blow?*
> *The small rain down can rain.*
> *Christ, if my love were in my arms,*
> *And I in my bed again!*

The impact of poetry is so hard and direct that for the moment there is no other sensation except that of the poem itself. What profound depths we visit then – how sudden and complete is our immersion! There is nothing here to catch hold of; nothing to stay us in our flight. The illusion of fiction is gradual; its effects are prepared; but who when they read these four lines stops to ask who wrote them, or conjures up the thought of Donne's house or Sidney's secretary; or enmeshes them in the intricacy of the past and the succession of generations? The poet is always our contemporary. Our being for the moment is centred and constricted, as in any violent shock of personal emotion. Afterwards, it is true, the sensation begins to spread in wider rings through our minds;

remoter senses are reached; these begin to sound and to comment and we are aware of echoes and reflections. The intensity of poetry covers an immense range of emotion. We have only to compare the force and directness of

> *I shall fall like a tree, and find my grave,*
>   *Only remembering that I grieve,*

with the wavering modulation of

> *Minutes are numbered by the fall of sands,*
> *As by an hour glass; the span of time*
> *Doth waste us to our graves, and we look on it;*
> *An age of pleasure, revelled out, comes home*
> *At last, and ends in sorrow; but the life,*
> *Weary of riot, numbers every sand,*
> *Wailing in sighs, until the last drop down,*
> *So to conclude calamity in rest,*

or place the meditative calm of

>   *whether we be young or old,*
> *Our destiny, our being's heart and home,*
> *Is with infinitude, and only there;*
> *With hope it is, hope that can never die,*
> *Effort, and expectation, and desire,*
> *And something evermore about to be,*

beside the complete and inexhaustible loveliness of

> *The moving Moon went up the sky,*
> *And nowhere did abide:*
> *Softly she was going up,*
> *And a star or two beside –*

or the splendid fantasy of

> *And the woodland haunter*
> *Shall not cease to saunter*
>   *When, far down some glade,*
> *Of the great world's burning,*
> *One soft flame upturning*
> *Seems, to his discerning,*
>   *Crocus in the shade,*

to bethink us of the varied art of the poet; his power to make us at once actors and spectators; his power to run his hand into character as if it were a glove, and be Falstaff or Lear; his power to condense, to widen, to state, once and for ever.

'We have only to compare' – with those words the cat is out of the bag, and the true complexity of reading is admitted. The first process, to receive impressions with the utmost understanding, is only half the process of reading; it must be completed, if we are to get the whole pleasure from a book, by another. We must pass judgment upon these multitudinous impressions; we must make of these fleeting shapes one that is hard and lasting. But not directly. Wait for the dust of reading to settle; for the conflict and the questioning to die down; walk, talk, pull the dead petals from a rose, or fall asleep. Then suddenly without our willing it, for it is thus that Nature undertakes these transitions, the book will return, but differently. It will float to the top of the mind as a whole. And the book as a whole is different from the book received currently in separate phrases. Details now fit themselves into their places. We see the shape from start to finish; it is a barn, a pig-sty, or a cathedral. Now then we can compare book with book as we compare building with building. But this act of comparison means that our attitude has changed; we are no longer the friends of the writer, but his judges; and just as we cannot be too sympathetic as friends, so as judges we cannot be too severe. Are they not criminals, books that have wasted our time and sympathy; are they not the most insidious enemies of society, corrupters, defilers, the writers of false books, faked books, books that fill the air with decay and disease? Let us then be severe in our judgments; let us compare each book with the greatest of its kind. There they hang in the mind, the shapes of the books we have read solidified by the judgments we have passed on them – *Robinson Crusoe, Emma, The Return of the Native.* Compare the novels with these – even the latest and least of novels has a right to be judged with the best. And so with poetry – when the intoxication of rhythm has died down and the splendour of words has faded, a

visionary shape will return to us and this must be compared
with *Lear*, with *Phèdre*, with *The Prelude*; or if not with these,
with whatever is the best or seems to us to be the best in its
own kind. And we may be sure that the newness of new poetry
and fiction is its most superficial quality and that we have
only to alter slightly, not to recast, the standards by which we
have judged the old.

It would be foolish, then, to pretend that the second part of
reading, to judge, to compare, is as simple as the first – to
open the mind wide to the fast flocking of innumerable impressions. To continue reading without the book before you,
to hold one shadow-shape against another, to have read
widely enough and with enough understanding to make such
comparisons alive and illuminating – that is difficult; it is still
more difficult to press further and to say, 'Not only is the
book of this sort, but it is of this value; here it fails; here it
succeeds; this is bad; that is good.' To carry out this part of a
reader's duty needs such imagination, insight, and learning
that it is hard to conceive any one mind sufficiently endowed;
impossible for the most self-confident to find more than the
seeds of such powers in himself. Would it not be wiser, then,
to remit this part of reading and to allow the critics, the
gowned and furred authorities of the library, to decide the
question of the book's absolute value for us? Yet how impossible! We may stress the value of sympathy; we may try to
sink our own identity as we read. But we know that we cannot
sympathize wholly or immerse ourselves wholly; there is always a demon in us who whispers, 'I hate, I love', and we
cannot silence him. Indeed, it is precisely because we hate and
we love that our relation with the poets and novelists is so
intimate that we find the presence of another person intolerable. And even if the results are abhorrent and our judgments
are wrong, still our taste, the nerve of sensation that sends
shocks through us, is our chief illuminant; we learn through
feeling; we cannot suppress our own idiosyncrasy without
impoverishing it. But as time goes on perhaps we can train
our taste; perhaps we can make it submit to some control.

When it has fed greedily and lavishly upon books of all sorts
– poetry, fiction, history, biography – and has stopped reading and looked for long spaces upon the variety, the incon-
gruity of the living world, we shall find that it is changing a
little; it is not so greedy, it is more reflective. It will begin to
bring us not merely judgments on particular books, but it will
tell us that there is a quality common to certain books. Listen,
it will say, what shall we call *this*? And it will read us perhaps
Lear and then perhaps the *Agamemnon* in order to bring out
that common quality. Thus, with our taste to guide us, we
shall venture beyond the particular book in search of qualities
that group books together; we shall give them names and thus
frame a rule that brings order into our perceptions. We shall
gain a further and a rarer pleasure from that discrimination.
But as a rule only lives when it is perpetually broken by contact with the books themselves – nothing is easier and more
stultifying than to make rules which exist out of touch with
facts, in a vacuum – now at last, in order to steady ourselves
in this difficult attempt, it may be well to turn to the very rare
writers who are able to enlighten us upon literature as an art.
Coleridge and Dryden and Johnson, in their considered criticism, the poets and novelists themselves in their unconsidered
sayings, are often surprisingly relevant; they light up and
solidify the vague ideas that have been tumbling in the misty
depths of our minds. But they are only able to help us if we
come to them laden with questions and suggestions won
honestly in the course of our own reading. They can do nothing for us if we herd ourselves under their authority and lie
down like sheep in the shade of a hedge. We can only understand their ruling when it comes in conflict with our own and
vanquishes it.

If this is so, if to read a book as it should be read calls for
the rarest qualities of imagination, insight, and judgment, you
may perhaps conclude that literature is a very complex art
and that it is unlikely that we shall be able, even after a life-
time of reading, to make any valuable contribution to its
criticism. We must remain readers; we shall not put on the

further glory that belongs to those rare beings who are also critics. But still we have our responsibilities as readers and even our importance. The standards we raise and the judgments we pass steal into the air and become part of the atmosphere which writers breathe as they work. An influence is created which tells upon them even if it never finds its way into print. And that influence, if it were well instructed, vigorous and individual and sincere, might be of great value now when criticism is necessarily in abeyance; when books pass in review like the procession of animals in a shooting gallery, and the critic has only one second in which to load and aim and shoot and may well be pardoned if he mistakes rabbits for tigers, eagles for barndoor fowls, or misses altogether and wastes his shot upon some peaceful cow grazing in a further field. If behind the erratic gunfire of the press the author felt that there was another kind of criticism, the opinion of people reading for the love of reading, slowly and unprofessionally, and judging with great sympathy and yet with great severity, might this not improve the quality of his work? And if by our means books were to become stronger, richer, and more varied, that would be an end worth reaching.

Yet who reads to bring about an end, however desirable? Are there not some pursuits that we practise because they are good in themselves, and some pleasures that are final? And is not this among them? I have sometimes dreamt, at least, that when the Day of Judgment dawns and the great conquerors and lawyers and statesmen come to receive their rewards – their crowns, their laurels, their names carved indelibly upon imperishable marble – the Almighty will turn to Peter and will say, not without a certain envy when He sees us coming with our books under our arms, 'Look, these need no reward. We have nothing to give them here. They have loved reading.'

1932

GEORGE ORWELL (1903–1950)

Politics and the English Language

Most people who bother with the matter at all would admit that the English language is in a bad way, but it is generally assumed that we cannot by conscious action do anything about it. Our civilization is decadent and our language – so the argument runs – must inevitably share in the general collapse. It follows that any struggle against the abuse of language is a sentimental archaism, like preferring candles to electric light or hansom cabs to aeroplanes. Underneath this lies the half-conscious belief that language is a natural growth and not an instrument which we shape for our own purposes.

Now, it is clear that the decline of a language must ultimately have political and economic causes: it is not due simply to the bad influence of this or that individual writer. But an effect can become a cause, reinforcing the original cause and producing the same effect in an intensified form, and so on indefinitely. A man may take to drink because he feels himself to be a failure, and then fail all the more completely because he drinks. It is rather the same thing that is happening to the English language. It becomes ugly and inaccurate because our thoughts are foolish, but the slovenliness of our language makes it easier for us to have foolish thoughts. The point is that the process is reversible. Modern English, especially written English, is full of bad habits which spread by imitation and which can be avoided if one is willing to take the necessary trouble. If one gets rid of these habits one can think more clearly, and to think clearly is a necessary first step towards political regeneration: so that the fight against bad English is not frivolous and is not the exclusive concern of professional writers. I will come back to this presently, and I hope that by that time the meaning of what I have said here will have become clearer. Meanwhile, here are five specimens of the English language as it is now habitually written.

Frye

amns struct. of essay

These five passages have not been picked out because they are especially bad – I could have quoted far worse if I had chosen – but because they illustrate various of the mental vices from which we now suffer. They are a little below the average, but are fairly representative samples. I number them so that I can refer back to them when necessary:

[1] I am not, indeed, sure whether it is not true to say that the Milton who once seemed not unlike a seventeenth-century Shelley had not become, out of an experience ever more bitter in each year, more alien [*sic*] to the founder of that Jesuit sect which nothing could induce him to tolerate.
PROFESSOR HAROLD LASKI
Essay in 'Freedom of Expression'

[2] Above all, we cannot play ducks and drakes with a native battery of idioms which prescribes such egregious collocations of vocables as the Basic *put up with* for *tolerate* or *put at a loss* for *bewilder*.
PROFESSOR LANCELOT HOGBEN
'Interglossa'

[3] On the one side we have the free personality: by definition it is not neurotic, for it has neither conflict nor dream. Its desires, such as they are, are transparent, for they are just what institutional approval keeps in the forefront of consciousness; another institutional pattern would alter their number and intensity; there is little in them that is natural, irreducible, or culturally dangerous. But *on the other side*,

the social bond itself is nothing but the mutual reflection of these self-secure integrities. Recall the definition of love. Is not this the very picture of a small academic? Where is there a place in this hall of mirrors for either personality or fraternity?

Essay on psychology in 'Politics' (New York)

[4] All the 'best people' from the gentlemen's clubs, and all the frantic fascist captains, united in common hatred of Socialism and bestial horror of the rising tide of the mass revolutionary movement, have turned to acts of provocation, to foul incendiarism, to medieval legends of poisoned wells, to legalize their own destruction of proletarian organizations, and rouse the agitated petty-bourgeoisie to chauvinistic fervour on behalf of the fight against the revolutionary way out of the crises.

Communist pamphlet

[5] If a new spirit *is* to be infused into this old country, there is one thorny and contentious reform which must be tackled, and that is the humanization and galvanization of the B.B.C. Timidity here will bespeak cancer and atrophy of the soul. The heart of Britain may be sound and of strong beat, for instance, but the British lion's roar at present is like that of Bottom in Shakespeare's *Midsummer Night's Dream* – as gentle as any sucking dove. A virile new Britain cannot continue indefinitely to be traduced in the eyes, or rather ears, of the world by the effete languors of Langham Place, brazenly masquerading as 'standard English'. When the Voice of Britain is heard at nine o'clock, better far and infinitely less ludicrous to hear aitches honestly dropped than the present priggish, inflated, inhibited, school-ma'amish arch braying of blameless bashful mewing maidens!

Letter in 'Tribune'

Each of these passages has faults of its own, but, quite apart from avoidable ugliness, two qualities are common to all of them. The first is staleness of imagery: the other is lack of precision. The writer either has a meaning and cannot express it, or he inadvertently says something else, or he is almost indifferent as to whether his words mean anything or not. This mixture of vagueness and sheer incompetence is the most marked characteristic of modern English prose, and especially of any kind of political writing. As soon as certain topics are raised, the concrete melts into the abstract and no one seems able to think of turns of speech that are not hackneyed: prose consists less and less of *words* chosen for the sake of their meaning, and more and more of *phrases* tacked together like the sections of a prefabricated hen-house. I list, below, with notes and examples, various of the tricks by means of which the work of prose-construction is habitually dodged:

DYING METAPHORS. A newly invented metaphor assists thought by evoking a visual image, while on the other hand a metaphor which is technically 'dead' (e.g. *iron resolution*) has in effect reverted to being an ordinary word and can generally be used without loss of vividness. But in between these two classes there is a huge dump of worn-out metaphors which have lost all evocative power and are merely used because they save people the trouble of inventing phrases for themselves. Examples are: *Ring the changes on, take up the cudgels for, toe the line, ride roughshod over, stand shoulder to shoulder with, play into the hands of, no axe to grind, grist to the mill, fishing in troubled waters, on the order of the day, Achilles' heel, swan song, hotbed.* Many of these are used without knowledge of their meaning (what is a 'rift', for instance?), and incompatible metaphors are frequently mixed, a sure sign that the writer is not interested in what he is saying. Some metaphors now current have been twisted out of their original meaning without those who use them even being aware of the fact. For example, *toe the line* is sometimes written *tow the line*. Another example is *the hammer and the anvil*, now always used with the implication that the anvil gets the worst of it.

In real life it is always the anvil that breaks the hammer, never the other way about: a writer who stopped to think what he was saying would be aware of this, and would avoid perverting the original phrase.

OPERATORS or VERBAL FALSE LIMBS. These save the trouble of picking out appropriate verbs and nouns, and at the same time pad each sentence with extra syllables which give it an appearance of symmetry. Characteristic phrases are: *render inoperative, militate against, make contact with, be subjected to, give rise to, give grounds for, have the effect of, play a leading part (role) in, make itself felt, take effect, exhibit a tendency to, serve the purpose of, etc., etc.* The keynote is the elimination of simple verbs. Instead of being a single word, such as *break, stop, spoil, mend, kill,* a verb becomes a *phrase,* made up of a noun or adjective tacked on to some general-purpose verb such as *prove, serve, form, play, render.* In addition, the passive voice is wherever possible used in preference to the active, and noun constructions are used instead of gerunds (*by examination of* instead of *by examining*). The range of verbs is further cut down by means of the *-ize* and *de-* formation, and the banal statements are given an appearance of profundity by means of the *not un-* formation. Simple conjunctions and prepositions are replaced by such phrases as *with respect to, having regard to, the fact that, by dint of, in view of, in the interests of, on the hypothesis that,* and the ends of sentences are saved from anticlimax by such resounding commonplaces as *greatly to be desired, cannot be left out of account, a development to be expected in the near future, deserving of serious consideration, brought to a satisfactory conclusion,* and so on and so forth.

PRETENTIOUS DICTION. Words like *phenomenon, element, individual* (as noun), *objective, categorical, effective, virtual, basic, primary, promote, constitute, exhibit, exploit, utilize, eliminate, liquidate,* are used to dress up simple statements and give an air of scientific impartiality to biased judgments. Adjectives like *epoch-making, epic, historic, unforgettable, triumphant, age-old, inevitable, inexorable, veritable,* are used to dignify the sordid processes of international politics, while writing that aims at glorifying war usually takes on an archaic colour, its characteristic words being: *realm, throne, chariot, mailed fist, trident, sword, shield, buckler, banner, jackboot, clarion.* Foreign words and expressions such as *cul de sac, ancien régime, deus ex machina, mutatis mutandis, status quo, gleichschaltung, weltanschauung,* are used to give an air of culture and elegance. Except for the useful abbreviations *i.e., e.g.,* and *etc.,* there is no real need for any of the hundreds of foreign phrases now current in English. Bad writers, and especially scientific, political and sociological writers, are nearly always haunted by the notion that Latin or Greek words are grander than Saxon ones, and unnecessary words like *expedite, ameliorate, predict, extraneous, deracinated, clandestine, subaqueous* and hundreds of others constantly gain ground from their Anglo-Saxon opposite numbers. The jargon peculiar to Marxist writing (*hyena, hangman, cannibal, petty bourgeois, these gentry, lacquey, flunkey, mad dog, White Guard,* etc.) consists largely of words and phrases translated from Russian, German or French; but the normal way of coining a new word is to use a Latin or Greek root with the appropriate affix and, where necessary, the *-ize* formation. It is often easier to make up words of this kind (*deregionalize, impermissible, extramarital, non-fragmentatory* and so forth) than to think up the English words that will cover one's meaning. The result, in general, is an increase in slovenliness and vagueness.

MEANINGLESS WORDS. In certain kinds of writing, particularly in art criticism and literary criticism, it is normal to come across long passages which are almost completely lacking in meaning. Words like *romantic, plastic, values, human, dead, sentimental, natural, vitality,* as used in art criticism, are strictly meaningless in the sense that they not only do not point to any discoverable object, but are hardly ever expected to do so by the reader. When one critic writes, 'The outstanding feature of Mr. X's work is its living quality', while another writes, 'The immediately striking thing about Mr. X's work is its peculiar deadness', the reader accepts this as a simple difference of opinion. If words like *black* and *white* were involved, instead of the jargon words *dead* and *living*, he would see at once that language was being used in an improper way. Many political words are similarly abused. The word *Fascism* has now no meaning except in so far as it signifies 'something not desirable'. The words *democracy, socialism, freedom, patriotic, realistic, justice*, have each of them several different meanings which cannot be reconciled with one another. In the case of a word like *democracy*, not only is there no agreed definition, but the attempt to make one is resisted from all sides. It is almost universally felt that when we call a country democratic we are praising it: consequently the defenders of every kind of régime claim that it is a democracy, and fear that they might have to stop using the word if it were tied down to any one meaning. Words of this kind are often used in a consciously dishonest way. That is, the person who uses them has his own private definition, but allows his hearer to think he means something quite different. Statements like *Marshal Pétain was a true patriot, The Soviet Press is the freest in the world, The Catholic Church is opposed to persecution*, are almost always made with intent to deceive. Other words used in variable meanings, in most cases more or less dishonestly, are: *class, totalitarian, science, progressive, reactionary, bourgeois, equality*.

Now that I have made this catalogue of swindles and perversions, let me give another example of the kind of writing that they lead to. This time it must of its nature be an imaginary one. I am going to translate a passage of good English into modern English of the worst sort. Here is a well-known verse from *Ecclesiastes:*

'I returned and saw under the sun, that the race is not to the swift, nor the battle to the strong, neither yet bread to the wise, nor yet riches to men of understanding, nor yet favour to men of skill; but time and chance happeneth to them all.'

Here it is in modern English:

'Objective consideration of contemporary phenomena compels the conclusion that success or failure in competitive activities exhibits no tendency to be commensurate with innate capacity, but that a considerable element of the unpredictable must invariably be taken into account.'

This is a parody, but not a very gross one. Exhibit (3), above, for instance, contains several patches of the same kind of English. It will be seen that I have not made a full translation. The beginning and ending of the sentence follow the original meaning fairly closely, but in the middle the concrete illustrations – race, battle, bread – dissolve into the vague phrase 'success or failure in competitive activities'. This had to be so, because no modern writer of the kind I am discussing – no one capable of using phrases like 'objective consideration of contemporary phenomena' – would ever tabulate his thoughts in that precise and detailed way. The whole tendency of modern prose is away from concreteness. Now analyse these two sentences a little more closely. The first contains forty-nine words but only sixty syllables, and all its words are those of everyday life. The second contains thirty-eight words of ninety syllables: eighteen of its words are from Latin roots, and one from Greek. The first sentence contains six vivid images, and only one phrase ('time and chance') that could be called vague. The second contains not a single fresh, arresting phrase, and in spite of its ninety syllables it gives only a shortened version of the meaning contained in the first. Yet without a doubt it is the second kind of sentence that is gaining ground in modern English. I do not want to exaggerate. This kind of writing is not yet universal, and outcrops of simplicity will occur here and there in the worst-written page. Still, if you or I were told to write a few lines on the uncertainty of human fortunes, we should probably come much nearer to my imaginary sentence than to the one from *Ecclesiastes*.

As I have tried to show, modern writing at its worst does not consist in picking out words for the sake of their meaning and inventing images in order to make the meaning clearer.

It consists in gumming together long strips of words which have already been set in order by someone else, and making the results presentable by sheer humbug. The attraction of this way of writing is that it is easy. It is easier – even quicker, once you have the habit – to say *In my opinion it is a not unjustifiable assumption that* than to say *I think*. If you use ready-made phrases, you not only don't have to hunt about for words; you also don't have to bother with the rhythms of your sentences, since these phrases are generally so arranged as to be more or less euphonious. When you are composing in a hurry – when you are dictating to a stenographer, for instance, or making a public speech – it is natural to fall into a pretentious, Latinized style. Tags like *a consideration which we should do well to bear in mind* or *a conclusion to which all of us would readily assent* will save many a sentence from coming down with a bump. By using stale metaphors, similes and idioms, you save much mental effort, at the cost of leaving your meaning vague, not only for your reader but for yourself. This is the significance of mixed metaphors. The sole aim of a metaphor is to call up a visual image. When these images clash – as in *The Fascist octopus has sung its swan song, the jackboot is thrown into the melting pot* – it can be taken as certain that the writer is not seeing a mental image of the objects he is naming; in other words he is not really thinking. Look again at the examples I gave at the beginning of this essay. Professor Laski (1) uses five negatives in fifty-three words. One of these is superfluous, making nonsense of the whole passage, and in addition there is the slip *alien* for akin, making further nonsense, and several avoidable pieces of clumsiness which increase the general vagueness. Professor Hogben (2) plays ducks and drakes with a battery which is able to write prescriptions, and, while disapproving of the everyday phrase *put up with*, is unwilling to look *egregious* up in the dictionary and see what it means. (3), if one takes an uncharitable attitude towards it, is simply meaningless: probably one could work out its intended meaning by reading the whole of the article in which it occurs. In (4), the writer knows more or less what he wants to say, but an accumulation of stale phrases chokes him like tea leaves blocking a sink. In (5), words and meaning have almost parted company. People who write in this manner usually have a general emotional meaning – they dislike one thing and want to express solidarity with another – but they are not interested in the detail of what they are saying. A scrupulous writer, in every sentence that he writes, will ask himself at least four questions, thus: What am I trying to say? What words will express it? What image or idiom will make it clearer? Is this image fresh enough to have an effect? And he will probably ask himself two more: Could I put it more shortly? Have I said anything that is avoidably ugly? But you are not obliged to go to all this trouble. You can shirk it by simply throwing your mind open and letting the ready-made phrases come crowding in. They will construct your sentences for you – even think your thoughts for you, to a certain extent – and at need they will perform the important service of partially concealing your meaning even from yourself. It is at this point that the special connection between politics and the debasement of language becomes clear.

In our time it is broadly true that political writing is bad writing. Where it is not true, it will generally be found that the writer is some kind of rebel, expressing his private opinions and not a 'party line'. Orthodoxy, of whatever colour, seems to demand a lifeless, imitative style. The political dialects to be found in pamphlets, leading articles, manifestos, White Papers and the speeches of under-secretaries do, of course, vary from party to party, but they are all alike in that one almost never finds in them a fresh, vivid, home-made turn of speech. When one watches some tired hack on the platform mechanically repeating the familiar phrases – *bestial atrocities, iron heel, bloodstained tyranny, free peoples of the world, stand shoulder to shoulder* – one often has a curious feeling that one is not watching a live human being but some kind of dummy: a feeling which suddenly becomes stronger at moments when the light catches the speaker's spectacles and turns them into blank discs which seem to have no eyes behind them. And this is not altogether fanciful. A speaker who uses that kind of phraseology has gone some distance towards turning himself into a machine. The appropriate noises are coming out of his larynx, but his brain is not involved as it would be if he were choosing his words for himself. If the speech he is making is one that he is accustomed to make over and over again, he may be almost unconscious of what he is saying, as one is when one utters the responses in church. And this reduced state of consciousness, if not indispensable, is at any rate favourable to political conformity.

In our time, political speech and writing are largely the defence of the indefensible. Things like the continuance of British rule in India, the Russian purges and deportations, the dropping of the atom bombs on Japan, can indeed be defended, but only by arguments which are too brutal for most people to face, and which do not square with the professed aims of political parties. Thus political language has to consist largely of euphemism, question-begging and sheer cloudy vagueness. Defenceless villages are bombarded from the air, the inhabitants driven out into the countryside, the cattle machine-gunned, the huts set on fire with incendiary bullets: this is called *pacification*. Millions of peasants are robbed of their farms and sent trudging along the roads with no more than they can carry: this is called *transfer of population* or *rectification of frontiers*. People are imprisoned for years without trial, or shot in the back of the neck or sent to die of scurvy in Arctic lumber camps: this is called *elimination of unreliable elements*. Such phraseology is needed if one wants to name things without calling up mental pictures of them. Consider for instance some comfortable English professor defending Russian totalitarianism. He cannot say outright, 'I believe in killing off your opponents when you can get good results by doing so.' Probably, therefore, he will say something like this:

'While freely conceding that the Soviet régime exhibits certain features which the humanitarian may be inclined to deplore, we must, I think, agree that a certain curtailment of the right to political opposition is an unavoidable concomitant of transitional periods, and that the rigours which the Russian people have been called upon to undergo have been amply justified in the sphere of concrete achievement.'

The inflated style is itself a kind of euphemism. A mass of Latin words falls upon the facts like soft snow, blurring the outlines and covering up all the details. The great enemy of clear language is insincerity. When there is a gap between one's real and one's declared aims, one turns as it were instinctively to long words and exhausted idioms, like a cuttlefish squirting out ink. In our age there is no such thing as 'keeping out of politics'. All issues are political issues, and politics itself is a mass of lies, evasions, folly, hatred and schizophrenia. When the general atmosphere is bad, language must suffer. I should expect to find – this is a guess which I have not sufficient knowledge to verify – that the German, Russian and Italian languages have all deteriorated in the last ten or fifteen years, as a result of dictatorship.

But if thought corrupts language, language can also corrupt thought. A bad usage can spread by tradition and imitation, even among people who should and do know better. The debased language that I have been discussing is in some ways very convenient. Phrases like *a not unjustifiable assumption, leaves much to be desired, would serve no good purpose, a consideration which we should do well to bear in mind*, are a continuous temptation, a packet of aspirins always at one's elbow. Look back through this essay, and for certain you will find that I have again and again committed the very faults I am protesting against. By this morning's post I have received a pamphlet dealing with conditions in Germany. The author tells me that he 'felt impelled' to write it. I open it at random, and here is almost the first sentence that I see: '[The Allies] have an opportunity not only of achieving a radical transformation of Germany's social and political structure in such a way as to avoid a nationalistic reaction in Germany itself, but at the same time of laying the foundations of a co-opera-

tive and unified Europe.' You see, he 'feels impelled' to write
– feels, presumably, that he has something new to say – and
yet his words, like cavalry horses answering the bugle, group
themselves automatically into the familiar dreary pattern.
This invasion of one's mind by ready-made phrases (*lay the
foundations, achieve a radical transformation*) can only be
prevented if one is constantly on guard against them, and
every such phrase anaesthetizes a portion of one's brain.

I said earlier that the decadence of our language is probably
curable. Those who deny this would argue, if they produced an
argument at all, that language merely reflects existing social
conditions, and that we cannot influence its development by
any direct tinkering with words and constructions. So far as
the general tone or spirit of a language goes, this may be true,
but it is not true in detail. Silly words and expressions have
often disappeared, not through any evolutionary process but
owing to the conscious action of a minority. Two recent examples were *explore every avenue* and *leave no stone unturned*,
which were killed by the jeers of a few journalists. There is a
long list of flyblown metaphors which could similarly be got
rid of if enough people would interest themselves in the job;
and it should also be possible to laugh the *not un-* formation
out of existence, to reduce the amount of Latin and Greek in
the average sentence, to drive out foreign phrases and strayed
scientific words, and, in general, to make pretentiousness un-
fashionable. But all these are minor points. The defence of the
English language implies more than this, and perhaps it is best
to start by saying what it does *not* imply.

To begin with it has nothing to do with archaism, with the
salvaging of obsolete words and turns of speech, or with the
setting up of a 'standard English' which must never be de-
parted from. On the contrary, it is especially concerned with
the scrapping of every word or idiom which has outworn its
usefulness. It has nothing to do with correct grammar and
syntax, which are of no importance so long as one makes one's
meaning clear, or with the avoidance of Americanisms, or
with having what is called a 'good prose style'. On the other

hand it is not concerned with fake simplicity and the attempt to make written English colloquial. Nor does it even imply in every case preferring the Saxon word to the Latin one, though it does imply using the fewest and shortest words that will cover one's meaning. What is above all needed is to let the meaning choose the word, and not the other way about. In prose, the worst thing one can do with words is to surrender to them. When you think of a concrete object, you think wordlessly, and then, if you want to describe the thing you have been visualizing you probably hunt about till you find the exact words that seem to fit. When you think of something abstract you are more inclined to use words from the start, and unless you make a conscious effort to prevent it, the existing dialect will come rushing in and do the job for you, at the expense of blurring or even changing your meaning. Probably it is better to put off using words as long as possible and get one's meaning as clear as one can through pictures or sensations. Afterwards one can choose – not simply *accept* – the phrases that will best cover the meaning, and then switch round and decide what impression one's words are likely to make on another person. This last effort of the mind cuts out all stale or mixed images, all prefabricated phrases, needless repetitions, and humbug and vagueness generally. But one can often be in doubt about the effect of a word or a phrase, and one needs rules that one can rely on when instinct fails. I think the following rules will cover most cases:

(i) Never use a metaphor, simile or other figure of speech which you are used to seeing in print.

(ii) Never use a long word where a short one will do.

(iii) If it is possible to cut a word out, always cut it out.

(iv) Never use the passive where you can use the active.

(v) Never use a foreign phrase, a scientific word or a jargon word if you can think of an everyday English equivalent.

(vi) Break any of these rules sooner than say anything outright barbarous.

These rules sound elementary, and so they are, but they demand a deep change of attitude in anyone who has grown used to writing in the style now fashionable. One could keep all of them and still write bad English, but one could not write the kind of stuff that I quoted in those five specimens at the beginning of this article.

I have not here been considering the literary use of language, but merely language as an instrument for expressing and not for concealing or preventing thought. Stuart Chase and others have come near to claiming that all abstract words are meaningless, and have used this as a pretext for advocating a kind of political quietism. Since you don't know what Fascism is, how can you struggle against Fascism? One need not swallow such absurdities as this, but one ought to recognize that the present political chaos is connected with the decay of language, and that one can probably bring about some improvement by starting at the verbal end. If you simplify your English, you are freed from the worst follies of orthodoxy. You cannot speak any of the necessary dialects, and when you make a stupid remark its stupidity will be obvious, even to yourself. Political language – and with variations this is true of all political parties, from Conservatives to Anarchists – is designed to make lies sound truthful and murder respectable, and to give an appearance of solidity to pure wind. One cannot change this all in a moment, but one can at least change one's own habits, and from time to time one can even, if one jeers loudly enough, send some worn-out and useless phrase – some *jackboot*, *Achilles' heel*, *hotbed*, *melting pot*, *acid test*, *veritable inferno* or other lump of verbal refuse – into the dustbin where it belongs.

1946

BERTRAND RUSSELL (b.1872)

In Praise of Idleness

Like most of my generation, I was brought up on the saying: 'Satan finds some mischief still for idle hands to do.' Being a highly virtuous child, I believed all that I was told, and acquired a conscience which has kept me working hard down to the present moment. But although my conscience has controlled my *actions*, my *opinions* have undergone a revolution. I think that there is far too much work done in the world, that immense harm is caused by the belief that work is virtuous, and that what needs to be preached in modern industrial countries is quite different from what always has been preached. Everyone knows the story of the traveller in Naples who saw twelve beggars lying in the sun (it was before the days of Mussolini), and offered a lira to the laziest of them. Eleven of them jumped up to claim it, so he gave it to the twelfth. This traveller was on the right lines. But in countries which do not enjoy Mediterranean sunshine idleness is more difficult, and a great public propaganda will be required to inaugurate it. I hope that, after reading the following pages, the leaders of the Y.M.C.A. will start a campaign to induce good young men to do nothing. If so, I shall not have lived in vain.

Before advancing my own arguments for laziness, I must dispose of one which I cannot accept. Whenever a person who already has enough to live on proposes to engage in some everyday kind of job, such as school-teaching or typing, he or she is told that such conduct takes the bread out of other people's mouths, and is therefore wicked. If this argument were valid, it would only be necessary for us all to be idle in order that we should all have our mouths full of bread. What people who say such things forget is that what a man earns he usually spends, and in spending he gives employment. As long as a man spends his income, he puts just as much bread into people's mouths in spending as he takes out of other people's mouths in earning. The real villain, from this point of view, is the man who saves. If he merely puts his savings in a stocking, like the proverbial French peasant, it is obvious that they do not give employment. If he invests his savings, the matter is less obvious, and different cases arise.

One of the commonest things to do with savings is to lend them to some Government. In view of the fact that the bulk of the public expenditure of most civilized Governments consists in payment for past wars or preparation for future wars, the man who lends his money to a Government is in the same position as the bad men in Shakespeare who hire murderers. The net result of the man's economical habits is to increase the armed forces of the State to which he lends his savings. Obviously it would be better if he spent the money, even if he spent it in drink or gambling.

But, I shall be told, the case is quite different when savings are invested in industrial enterprises. When such enterprises succeed, and produce something useful, this may be conceded. In these days, however, no one will deny that most enterprises fail. That means that a large amount of human labour, which might have been devoted to producing something that could be enjoyed, was expended on producing machines which, when produced, lay idle and did no good to anyone. The man who invests his savings in a concern that goes bankrupt is therefore injuring others as well as himself. If he spent his money, say, in giving parties for his friends, they (we may hope) would get pleasure, and so would all those upon whom he spent money, such as the butcher, the baker, and the bootlegger. But if he spends it (let us say) upon laying down rails for surface cars in some place where surface cars turn out to be not wanted, he has diverted a mass of labour into channels where it gives pleasure to no one. Nevertheless, when he becomes poor through the failure of his investment he will be regarded as a victim of undeserved misfortune, whereas the gay spendthrift, who has spent his money philanthropically, will be despised as a fool and a frivolous person.

All this is only preliminary. I want to say, in all seriousness, that a great deal of harm is being done in the modern world by belief in the virtuousness of WORK, and that the road to happiness and prosperity lies in an organized diminution of work.

First of all: what is work? Work is of two kinds: first, altering the position of matter at or near the earth's surface relatively to other such matter; second, telling other people to do so. The first kind is unpleasant and ill paid; the second is pleasant and highly paid. The second kind is capable of indefinite extension: there are not only those who give orders, but those who give advice as to what orders should be given. Usually two opposite kinds of advice are given simultaneously by two organized bodies of men; this is called politics. The skill required for this kind of work is not knowledge of the subjects as to which advice is given, but knowledge of the art of persuasive speaking and writing, i.e. of advertising.

Throughout Europe, though not in America, there is a third class of men, more respected than either of the classes of workers. There are men who, through ownership of land, are able to make others pay for the privilege of being allowed to exist and to work. These landowners are idle, and I might therefore be expected to praise them. Unfortunately, their idleness is only rendered possible by the industry of others; indeed their desire for comfortable idleness is historically the source of the whole gospel of work. The last thing they have ever wished is that others should follow their example.

From the beginning of civilization until the Industrial Revolution, a man could, as a rule, produce by hard work little more than was required for the subsistence of himself and his

BERTRAND RUSSELL

* Old notion of work a holdover

family, although his wife worked at least as hard as he did, and his children added their labour as soon as they were old enough to do so. The small surplus above bare necessaries was not left to those who produced it, but was appropriated by warriors and priests. In times of famine there was no surplus; the warriors and priests, however, still secured as much as at other times, with the result that many of the workers died of hunger. This system persisted in Russia until 1917, and still persists in the East; in England, in spite of the Industrial Revolution, it remained in full force throughout the Napoleonic wars, and until a hundred years ago, when the new class of manufacturers acquired power. In America, the system came to an end with the Revolution, except in the South, where it persisted until the Civil War. A system which lasted so long and ended so recently has naturally left a profound impress upon men's thoughts and opinions. Much that we take for granted about the desirability of work is derived from this system, and, being pre-industrial, is not adapted to the modern world. Modern technique has made it possible for leisure, within limits, to be not the prerogative of small privileged classes, but a right evenly distributed throughout the community. The morality of work is the morality of slaves, and the modern world has no need of slavery.

It is obvious that, in primitive communities, peasants, left to themselves, would not have parted with the slender surplus upon which the warriors and priests subsisted, but would have either produced less or consumed more. At first, sheer force compelled them to produce and part with the surplus. Gradually, however, it was found possible to induce many of them to accept an ethic according to which it was their duty to work hard, although part of their work went to support others in idleness. By this means the amount of compulsion required was lessened, and the expenses of government were diminished. To this day, ninety-nine per cent of British wage-earners would be genuinely shocked if it were proposed that the King should not have a larger income than a working man. The conception of duty, speaking historically, has been a means used by the holders of power to induce others to live for the interests of their masters rather than for their own. Of course the holders of power conceal this fact from themselves by managing to believe that their interests are identical with the larger interests of humanity. Sometimes this is true; Athenian slave-owners, for instance, employed part of their leisure in making a permanent contribution to civilization which would have been impossible under a just economic system. Leisure is essential to civilization, and in former times leisure for the few was only rendered possible by the labours of the many. But their labours were valuable, not because work is good, but because leisure is good. And with modern technique it would be possible to distribute leisure justly without injury to civilization.

Modern technique has made it possible to diminish enormously the amount of labour required to secure the necessaries of life for everyone. This was made obvious during the war. At that time, all the men in the armed forces, all the men and women engaged in the production of munitions, all the men and women engaged in spying, war propaganda, or Government offices connected with the war, were withdrawn from productive occupations. In spite of this, the general level of physical well-being among unskilled wage-earners on the side of the Allies was higher than before or since. The significance of this fact was concealed by finance: borrowing made it appear as if the future was nourishing the present. But that, of course, would have been impossible; a man cannot eat a loaf of bread that does not yet exist. The war showed conclusively that, by the scientific organization of production, it is possible to keep modern populations in fair comfort on a small part of the working capacity of the modern world. If, at the end of the war, the scientific organization, which had been created in order to liberate men for fighting and munition work, had been preserved, and the hours of work had been cut down to four, all would have been well. Instead of that the old chaos was restored, those whose work was demanded were made to work long hours, and the rest were left to starve as unemployed. Why? – because work is a duty, and a man should not receive wages in proportion to what he has produced, but in proportion to his virtue as exemplified by his industry.

This is the morality of the Slave State, applied in circumstances totally unlike those in which it arose. No wonder the result has been disastrous. Let us take an illustration. Suppose that, at a given moment, a certain number of people are engaged in the manufacture of pins. They make as many pins as the world needs, working (say) eight hours a day. Someone makes an invention by which the same number of men can make twice as many pins as before. But the world does not need twice as many pins: pins are already so cheap that hardly any more will be bought at a lower price. In a sensible world, everybody concerned in the manufacture of pins would take to working four hours instead of eight, and everything else would go on as before. But in the actual world this would be thought demoralizing. The men still work eight hours, there are too many pins, some employers go bankrupt, and half the men previously concerned in making pins are thrown out of work. There is, in the end, just as much leisure as on the other plan, but half the men are totally idle while half are still overworked. In this way, it is insured that the unavoidable leisure shall cause misery all round instead of being a universal source of happiness. Can anything more insane be imagined?

The idea that the poor should have leisure has always been shocking to the rich. In England, in the early nineteenth century, fifteen hours was the ordinary day's work for a man; children sometimes did as much, and very commonly did twelve hours a day. When meddlesome busybodies suggested that perhaps these hours were rather long, they were told that work kept adults from drink and children from mischief. When I was a child, shortly after urban working men had acquired the vote, certain public holidays were established by law, to the great indignation of the upper classes. I remember hearing an old Duchess say: 'What do the poor want with holidays? They ought to *work*.' People nowadays are less frank, but the sentiment persists, and is the source of much of our economic confusion.

Let us, for a moment, consider the ethics of work frankly, without superstition. Every human being, of necessity, consumes, in the course of his life, a certain amount of the produce of human labour. Assuming, as we may, that labour is on the whole disagreeable, it is unjust that a man should consume more than he produces. Of course he may provide services rather than commodities, like a medical man, for example; but he should provide something in return for his board and lodging. To this extent, the duty of work must be admitted, but to this extent only.

I shall not dwell upon the fact that, in all modern societies outside the U.S.S.R., many people escape even this minimum of work, namely all those who inherit money and all those who marry money. I do not think the fact that these people are allowed to be idle is nearly so harmful as the fact that wage-earners are expected to overwork or starve.

If the ordinary wage-earner worked four hours a day, there would be enough for everybody, and no unemployment – assuming a certain very moderate amount of sensible organization. This idea shocks the well-to-do, because they are convinced that the poor would not know how to use so much leisure. In America, men often work long hours even when they are already well off; such men, naturally, are indignant at the idea of leisure for wage-earners, except as the grim punishment of unemployment; in fact, they dislike leisure even for their sons. Oddly enough, while they wish their sons to work so hard as to have no time to be civilized, they do not mind their wives and daughters having no work at all. The snobbish admiration of uselessness, which, in an aristocratic society, extends to both sexes, is, under a plutocracy, confined to women; this, however, does not make it any more in agreement with common sense.

The wise use of leisure, it must be conceded, is a product of civilization and education. A man who has worked long hours all his life will be bored if he becomes suddenly idle. But without a considerable amount of leisure a man is cut off from many of the best things. There is no longer any reason why the bulk of the population should suffer this deprivation; only a foolish asceticism, usually vicarious, makes us continue to insist on work in excessive quantities now that the need no longer exists.

In the new creed which controls the government of Russia, while there is much that is very different from the traditional teaching of the West, there are some things that are quite unchanged. The attitude of the governing classes, and especially of those who conduct educational propaganda, on the subject of the dignity of labour, is almost exactly that which the governing classes of the world have always preached to what were called the 'honest poor'. Industry, sobriety, willingness to work long hours for distant advantages, even submissiveness to authority, all these reappear; moreover authority still represents the will of the Ruler of the Universe, who, however, is now called by a new name, Dialectical Materialism.

The victory of the proletariat in Russia has some points in common with the victory of the feminists in some other countries. For ages, men had conceded the superior saintliness of women, and had consoled women for their inferiority by maintaining that saintliness is more desirable than power. At last the feminists decided that they would have both, since the pioneers among them believed all that the men had told them about the desirability of virtue, but not what they had told them about the worthlessness of political power. A similar thing has happened in Russia as regards manual work. For ages, the rich and their sycophants have written in praise of 'honest toil', have praised the simple life, have professed a religion which teaches that the poor are much more likely to go to heaven than the rich, and in general have tried to make manual workers believe that there is some special nobility about altering the position of matter in space, just as men tried to make women believe that they derived some special nobility from their sexual enslavement. In Russia, all this teaching about the excellence of manual work has been taken seriously, with the result that the manual worker is more honoured than anyone else. What are, in essence, revivalist appeals are made, but not for the old purposes: they are made to secure shock workers for special tasks. Manual work is the ideal which is held before the young, and is the basis of all ethical teaching.

For the present, possibly, this is all to the good. A large country, full of natural resources, awaits development, and has to be developed with very little use of credit. In these circumstances, hard work is necessary, and is likely to bring a great reward. But what will happen when the point has been reached where everybody could be comfortable without working long hours?

In the West, we have various ways of dealing with this problem. We have no attempt at economic justice, so that a large proportion of the total produce goes to a small minority of the population, many of whom do no work at all. Owing to the absence of any central control over production, we produce hosts of things that are not wanted. We keep a large percentage of the working population idle, because we can dispense with their labour by making the others overwork. When all these methods prove inadequate, we have a war: we cause a number of people to manufacture high explosives, and a number of others to explode them, as if we were children who had just discovered fireworks. By a combination of all these devices we manage, though with difficulty, to keep alive the notion that a great deal of severe manual work must be the lot of the average man.

In Russia, owing to more economic justice and central control over production, the problem will have to be differently solved. The rational solution would be, as soon as the necessaries and elementary comforts can be provided for all, to reduce the hours of labour gradually, allowing a popular vote to decide, at each stage, whether more leisure or more goods were to be preferred. But, having taught the supreme virtue of hard work, it is difficult to see how the authorities can aim at a paradise in which there will be much leisure and little work. It seems more likely that they will find continually fresh schemes, by which present leisure is to be sacrificed to future productivity. I read recently of an ingenious plan put forward by Russian engineers, for making the White Sea and the Northern coasts of Siberia warm, by putting a dam across the Kara Sea. An admirable project, but liable to postpone proletarian comfort for a generation, while the nobility of toil is being displayed amid the ice-fields and snowstorms of the Arctic Ocean. This sort of thing, if it happens, will be the result of regarding the virtue of hard work as an end in itself, rather than as a means to a state of affairs in which it is no longer needed.

The fact is that moving matter about, while a certain amount of it is necessary to our existence, is emphatically not one of the ends of human life. If it were, we should have to consider every navvy superior to Shakespeare. We have been misled in this matter by two causes. One is the necessity of keeping the poor contented, which has led the rich, for thousands of years, to preach the dignity of labour, while taking care themselves to remain undignified in this respect. The other is the new pleasure in mechanism, which makes us delight in the astonishingly clever changes that we can produce on the earth's surface. Neither of these motives makes any great appeal to the actual worker. If you ask him what he thinks the best part of his life, he is not likely to say: 'I enjoy manual work because it makes me feel that I am fulfilling man's noblest task, and because I like to think how much man can transform his planet. It is true that my body demands periods of rest, which I have to fill in as best I may, but I am never so happy as when the morning comes and I can return to the toil from which my contentment springs.' I have never heard working men say this sort of thing. They consider work, as it should be considered, a necessary means to a livelihood, and it is from their leisure hours that they derive whatever happiness they may enjoy.

It will be said that, while a little leisure is pleasant, men would not know how to fill their days if they had only four hours of work out of the twenty-four. In so far as this is true in the modern world, it is a condemnation of our civilization; it would not have been true at any earlier period. There was formerly a capacity for light-heartedness and play which has been to some extent inhibited by the cult of efficiency. The modern man thinks that everything ought to be done for the sake of something else, and never for its own sake. Serious-minded persons, for example, are continually condemning the habit of going to the cinema, and telling us that it leads the young into crime. But all the work that goes to producing a cinema is respectable, because it is work, and because it brings a money profit. The notion that the desirable activities are those that bring a profit has made everything topsy-turvy. The butcher who provides you with meat and the baker who provides you with bread are praiseworthy, because they are making money; but when you enjoy the food they have provided, you are merely frivolous, unless you eat only to get strength for your work. Broadly speaking, it is held that getting money is good and spending money is bad. Seeing that they are two sides of one transaction, this is absurd; one might as well maintain that keys are good, but keyholes are bad. Whatever merit there may be in the production of goods must be entirely derivative from the advantage to be obtained by consuming them. The individual, in our society, works for profit; but the social purpose of his work lies in the consumption of what he produces. It is this divorce between the individual and the social purpose of production that makes it so difficult for men to think clearly in a world in which profit-making is the incentive to industry. We think too much of production, and too little of consumption. One result is that we attach too little importance to enjoyment and simple happiness, and that we do not judge production by the pleasure that it gives to the consumer.

When I suggest that working hours should be reduced to four, I am not meaning to imply that all the remaining time should necessarily be spent in pure frivolity. I mean that four hours' work a day should entitle a man to the necessities and elementary comforts of life, and that the rest of his time should be his to use as he might see fit. It is an essential part of any such social system that education should be carried further than it usually is at present, and should aim, in part, at providing tastes which would enable a man to use leisure intelligently. I am not thinking mainly of the sort of things that would be considered 'highbrow'. Peasant dances have died out except in remote rural areas, but the impulses which caused them to be cultivated must still exist in human nature. The pleasures of urban populations have become mainly passive: seeing cinemas, watching football matches, listening to the radio, and so on. This results from the fact that their active energies are fully taken up with work; if they had more leisure, they would again enjoy pleasures in which they took an active part.

In the past, there was a small leisure class and a larger working class. The leisure class enjoyed advantages for which there was no basis in social justice; this necessarily made it oppressive, limited its sympathies, and caused it to invent theories by which to justify its privileges. These facts greatly diminished its excellence, but in spite of this drawback it contributed nearly the whole of what we call civilization. It cultivated the arts and discovered the sciences; it wrote books, invented the philosophies, and refined social relations. Even the liberation of the oppressed has usually been inaugurated from above. Without the leisure class, mankind would never have emerged from barbarism.

The method of a hereditary leisure class without duties was, however, extraordinarily wasteful. None of the members of the class had been taught to be industrious, and the class as a whole was not exceptionally intelligent. The class might produce one Darwin, but against him had to be set tens of thousands of country gentlemen who never thought of anything more intelligent than fox-hunting and punishing poachers. At present, the universities are supposed to provide, in a more systematic way, what the leisure class provided accidentally and as a by-product. This is a great improvement, but it has certain drawbacks. University life is so different from life in the world at large that men who live in an academic *milieu* tend to be unaware of the preoccupations and problems of ordinary men and women; moreover their ways of expressing themselves are usually such as to rob their opinions of the influence that they ought to have upon the general public. Another disadvantage is that in universities studies are organized, and the man who thinks of some original line of research is likely to be discouraged. Academic institutions, therefore, useful as they are, are not adequate guardians of the interests of civilization in a world where everyone outside their walls is too busy for unutilitarian pursuits.

In a world where no one is compelled to work more than four hours a day, every person possessed of scientific curiosity will be able to indulge it, and every painter will be able to paint without starving, however excellent his pictures may be. Young writers will not be obliged to draw attention to themselves by sensational pot-boilers, with a view to acquiring the economic independence needed for monumental works, for which, when the time at last comes, they will have lost the taste and the capacity. Men who, in their professional work, have become interested in some phase of economics or government, will be able to develop their ideas without the academic detachment that makes the work of university economists often seem lacking in reality. Medical men will have time to learn about the progress of medicine, teachers will not be exasperatedly struggling to teach by routine methods things which they learnt in their youth, which may, in the interval, have been proved to be untrue.

Above all, there will be happiness and joy of life, instead of frayed nerves, weariness, and dyspepsia. The work exacted will be enough to make leisure delightful, but not enough to produce exhaustion. Since men will not be tired in their spare time, they will not demand only such amusements as are passive and vapid. At least one per cent will probably devote the time not spent in professional work to pursuits of some public importance, and, since they will not depend upon these pursuits for their livelihood, their originality will be unhampered, and there will be no need to conform to the standards set by elderly pundits. But it is not only in these exceptional cases that the advantages of leisure will appear. Ordinary men and women, having the opportunity of a happy life, will become more kindly and less persecuting and less inclined to view others with suspicion. The taste for war will die out, partly for this reason, and partly because it will involve long and severe work for all. Good nature is, of all moral qualities, the one that the world needs most, and good nature is the result of ease and security, not of a life of arduous struggle. Modern methods of production have given us the possibility of ease and security for all; we have chosen, instead, to have overwork for some and starvation for the others. Hitherto we have continued to be as energetic as we were before there were machines; in this we have been foolish, but there is no reason to go on being foolish for ever.

1932

HERBERT READ (b.1893)

To Hell with Culture

I write, not as a philistine, but as a man who could not only claim to be cultured in the accepted sense of the word, but who has actually devoted most of his life to cultural things – to the practice of the arts of the present and the elucidation of the arts of the past. My philosophy is a direct product of my aesthetic experience, and I believe that life without art would be a graceless and brutish existence. I could not live without the spiritual values of art. I know that some people are insensitive to these values, but before allowing myself to pity or despise such people, I try to imagine how they got themselves into such a poor state of mind. The more I consider such people, the more clearly I begin to perceive that though there may be a minority who have been hopelessly brutalized by their environment and upbringing, the great majority are not insensitive, but indifferent. They have sensibility, but the thing we call culture does not stir them. Architecture and sculpture, painting and poetry, are not the immediate concerns of their lives. They are therefore not sensibly moved by the baroque rhetoric of St. Paul's, or the painted ceiling of the Sistine Chapel, or any of the minor monuments of our culture. If they go into a museum or art gallery, they move about with dead eyes: they have strayed among people who do not speak their language, with whom they cannot by any means communicate.

Now the common assumption is that this strayed riveter, as we may call him, should set about it and learn the language of

this strange country – that he should attend museum lectures
and adult education classes in the little spare time he has, and
so gradually lift himself on to the cultured level. Our whole
educational system is built on that assumption, and very few
democrats would be found to question it. And yet a moment's
consideration should convince us that an educational system
which is built on such an assumption is fundamentally wrong,
and fundamentally undemocratic. Our riveter has probably
strayed from a cheerless street in Birmingham, where he in-
habits a mean little house furnished with such shoddy comforts
as he has been able to afford out of his inadequate wage. I need
not pursue the man's life in all its dreary detail: there he
stands, typical of millions of workers in this country, his
clumsy boots on the parquet floor, and you are asking him to
appreciate a painting by Botticelli or a bust by Bernini, a
Spanish textile or a fine piece of Limoges enamel. If drink is
the shortest road out of Manchester, there is a possibility that
art may be the shortest road out of Birmingham; but it will
not be a crowded road, and only a very odd and eccentric
worker will be found to respond to the aesthetic thrills that
run down a cultured spine.

There are cultured people who, realizing this fact, are honest enough to abandon their democratic pretensions – they
put up an impenetrable barrier between the people and art,
between the worker and 'culture'. It is much better, they say,
'that civilization should be retained in the hands of those
persons to whom it professionally belongs. Until they are
educated, and unless they are, it will be one worker in a million
who wants to read a modern poem.'

Such people are right, and such people are wrong. They are
right to assume that an impenetrable barrier exists between
their culture and the worker: they are wrong to imagine that
the worker has no cultural sensibility. The worker has as much
latent sensibility as any human being, but that sensibility can
only be awakened when meaning is restored to his daily work,
and he is allowed to create his own culture.

Do not let us be deceived by the argument that culture is

the same for all time – that art is a unity and beauty an absolute value. If you are going to talk about abstract conceptions like beauty, then we can freely grant that they are absolute and eternal. But abstract conceptions are not works of art. Works of art are things of use – houses and their furniture, for example; and if, like sculpture and poetry, they are not things of immediate use, then they should be things consonant with the things we use – that is to say, part of our daily life, tuned to our daily habits, accessible to our daily needs. It is not until art expresses the immediate hopes and aspirations of humanity that it acquires its social relevance.

A culture begins with simple things – with the way the potter moulds the clay on his wheel, the way a weaver threads his yarns, the way the builder builds his house. Greek culture did not begin with the Parthenon: it began with a whitewashed hut on a hillside. Culture has always developed as an infinitely slow but sure refinement and elaboration of simple things – refinement and elaboration of speech, refinement and elaboration of shapes, refinement and elaboration of proportions, with the original purity persisting right through. A democratic culture will begin in a *similar* way. We shall not revert to the peasant's hut or the potter's wheel. We shall begin with the elements of modern industry – electric power, metal alloys, cement, the tractor and the aeroplane. We shall consider these things as the raw materials of a civilization and we shall work out their appropriate use and appropriate forms, without reference to the lath and plaster of the past.

Today we are bound hand and foot to the past. Because property is a sacred thing and land values a source of untold wealth, our houses must be crowded together and our streets must follow their ancient illogical meanderings. Because houses must be built at the lowest possible cost to allow the highest possible profit, they are denied the art and science of the architect. Because everything we buy for use must be sold for profit, and because there must always be this profitable margin between cost and price, our pots and our pans, our furniture and our clothes, have the same shoddy consistency,

the same competitive cheapness. You know what a veneer is:
a paper-thin layer of rosewood or walnut glued to a frame-
work of pine or deal. The whole of our capitalist culture is one
immense veneer: a surface refinement hiding the cheapness
and shoddiness at the heart of things.

To hell with such a culture! To the rubbish-heap and furnace
with it all! Let us celebrate the democratic revolution with the
biggest holocaust in the history of the world. When Hitler has
finished bombing our cities, let the demolition squads complete the good work. Then let us go into the wide open spaces
and build anew.

Let us build cities that are not too big, but spacious, with
traffic flowing freely through their leafy avenues, with children
playing safely in their green and flowery parks, with people
living happily in bright efficient houses. Let us place our
factories and workshops where natural conditions of supply
make their location most convenient – the necessary electric
power can be laid on anywhere. Let us balance agriculture and
industry, town and country – let us do all these sensible and
elementary things and *then* let us talk about our culture.

A culture of pots and pans! some of my readers may cry
contemptuously. I do not despise a culture of pots and pans,
because as I have already said, the best civilizations of the past
may be judged by their pots and pans. But what I am now
asserting, as a law of history no less than as a principle of
social economy, is that until a society can produce beautiful
pots and pans as naturally as it grows potatoes, it will be
incapable of those higher forms of art which in the past have
taken the form of temples and cathedrals, epics and operas.

As for the past, let the past take care of itself. I know that
there is such a thing as tradition, but in so far as it is valuable
it is a body of technical knowledge – the mysteries of the old
guilds – and can safely be entrusted to the care of the new
guilds. There is a traditional way of thatching haystacks and
a traditional way of writing sonnets: they can be learned by
any apprentice. If I am told that this is not the profoundest
meaning of the word tradition, I will not be obtuse; but I will

merely suggest that the state of the world today is a sufficient comment on those traditional embodiments of wisdom, ecclesiastical or academic, which we are expected to honour. The cultural problem, we are told by these traditionalists, is at bottom a spiritual, even a religious one. But this is not true. At least, it is no truer of the cultural problem than of the economic problem, or any of the other problems which await the solution of the Democratic Order.

1941

— paragraphs

E. B. WHITE (b.1899)

tone
setting
the man
the issues

On a Florida Key

low island or reef

Setting   I am writing this in a beach cottage on a Florida key. It is
raining to beat the cars. The rollers from a westerly storm are
simple creaming along the shore, making a steady boiling noise in-
sentences stead of the usual intermittent slap. The Chamber of Commerce has drawn the friendly blind against this ugliness and
is busy getting out some advance notices of the style parade
which is to be held next Wednesday at the pavilion. The paper
says cooler tomorrow.

The walls of my room are of matched boarding, applied
horizontally and painted green. On the floor is a straw mat.
Under the mat is a layer of sand that has been tracked into the
Contempl cottage and has sifted through the straw. I have thought some
of taking the mat up and sweeping the sand into a pile and
removing it, but have decided against it. This is the way keys
form, apparently, and I have no particular reason to interfere.
On a small wooden base in one corner of the room is a gas
heater, supplied from a tank on the premises. This device can
raise the temperature of the room with great rapidity by con-
verting the oxygen of the air into heat. In deciding whether
to light the heater or leave it alone, one has only to choose
Freeze whether he wants to congeal in a well-ventilated room or
suffocate in comfort. After a little practice, a nice balance can
be established – enough oxygen left to sustain life, yet enough
heat generated to prevent death from exposure.

On the west wall hangs an Indian rug, and to one edge of

the rug is pinned a button which carries the legend: Junior Programs Joop Club. Built into the north wall is a cabinet made of pecky cypress. On the top shelf are three large pine cones, two of them painted emerald-green, the third painted brick-red. Also a gilded candlestick in the shape of a Roman chariot. Another shelf holds some shells which, at the expenditure of considerable effort on somebody's part, have been made to look like birds. On the bottom shelf is a tiny toy collie, made of rabbit fur, with a tongue of red flannel.

In the kitchenette just beyond where I sit is a gas stove and a small electric refrigerator of an ancient vintage. The ice trays show deep claw marks, where people have tried to pry them free, using can openers and knives and screwdrivers and petulance. When the refrigerator snaps on it makes a noise which can be heard all through the cottage and the lights everywhere go dim for a second and then return to their normal brilliancy. This refrigerator contains the milk, the butter, and the eggs for tomorrow's breakfast. More milk will arrive in the morning, but I will save it for use on the morrow, so that every day I shall use the milk of the previous day, never taking advantage of the opportunity to enjoy perfectly fresh milk. This is a situation which could be avoided if I had the guts to throw away a whole bottle of milk, but nobody has that much courage in the world today. It is a sin to throw away milk and we know it.

The water which flows from the faucets in the kitchen sink and in the bathroom contains sulphur and is not good to drink. It leaves deep-brown stains around the drains. Applied to the face with a shaving brush, it feels as though fine sandpaper were being drawn across your jowls. It is so hard and sulphurous that ordinary soap will not yield to it, and the breakfast dishes have to be washed with a washing powder known as Dreft.

On the porch of the cottage, each in a special stand, are two carboys of spring water – for drinking, making coffee, and brushing teeth. There is a deposit of two dollars on bottle and stand, and the water itself costs fifty cents. Two rival companies furnish water to the community, and I happened to get mixed up with both of them. Every couple of days a man from one or the other of the companies shows up and hangs around for a while, whining about the presence on my porch of the rival's carboy. I have made an attempt to dismiss one company and retain the other, but to accomplish it would require a dominant personality and I haven't one. I have been surprised to see how long it takes a man to drink up ten gallons of water. I should have thought I could have done it in half the time it has taken me.

This morning I read in the paper of an old Negro, one hundred and one years old, and he was boasting of the quantity of whisky he had drunk in his life. He said he had once worked in a distillery and they used to give him half a gallon of whisky a day to take home, which kept him going all right during the week, but on weekends, he said, he would have to buy a gallon extry, to tide him over till Monday.

In the kitchen cabinet is a bag of oranges for morning juice. Each orange is stamped 'Color Added'. The dyeing of an orange, to make it orange, is Man's most impudent gesture to date. It is really an appalling piece of effrontery, carrying the clear implication that Nature doesn't know what she is up to. I think an orange, dyed orange, is as repulsive as a pine cone painted green. I think it is about as ugly a thing as I have ever seen, and it seems hard to believe that here, within ten miles, probably, of the trees which bore the fruit, I can't buy an orange which somebody hasn't smeared with paint. But I doubt that there are many who feel that way about it, because fraudulence has become a national virtue and is well thought of in many circles. In the past twenty-four hours, I see by this morning's paper, one hundred and thirty-six cars of oranges have been shipped. There are probably millions of children today who have never seen a natural orange – only an artificially colored one. If they should see a natural orange they might think something had gone wrong with it.

There are two moving picture theaters in the town to which my key is attached by a bridge. In one of them colored people are allowed in the balcony. In the other, colored people are not allowed at all. I saw a patriotic newsreel there the other day which ended with a picture of the American flag blowing in the breeze, and the words: one nation indivisible, with liberty and justice for all. Everyone clapped, but I decided I could not clap for liberty and justice (for all) while I was in a theater from which Negroes had been barred. And I felt there were too many people in the world who think liberty and justice for all means liberty and justice for themselves and their friends. I sat there wondering what would happen to me if I were to jump up and say in a loud voice: 'If you folks like liberty and justice so much, why do you keep Negroes from this theater?' I am sure it would have surprised everybody very much and it is the kind of thing I dream about doing but never do. If I had done it I suppose the management would have taken me by the arm and marched me out of the theater, on the grounds that it is disturbing the peace to speak up for liberty just as the feature is coming on. When a man is in the South he must do as the Southerners do; but although I am willing to call my wife 'Sugar' I am not willing to call a colored person a nigger.

Northerners are quite likely to feel that Southerners are bigoted on the race question, and Southerners almost invariably figure that Northerners are without any practical experience and therefore their opinions aren't worth much. The Jim Crow philosophy of color is unsatisfying to a Northerner, but is regarded as sensible and expedient to residents of towns where the Negro population is as large as or larger than the white. Whether one makes a practical answer or an idealistic answer to a question depends partly on whether one is talking in terms of one year, or ten years, or a hundred years. It is, in other words, conceivable that the Negroes of a hundred years from now will enjoy a greater degree of liberty if the present restrictions on today's Negroes are not relaxed too fast. But that doesn't get today's Negroes in to see Hedy Lamarr.

I have to laugh when I think about the sheer inconsistency

celebration

of the Southern attitude about color: the Negro barred from the movie house because of color, the orange with 'color added' for its ultimate triumph. Some of the cities in this part of the State have fête days to commemorate the past and advertise the future, and in my mind I have been designing a float which I would like to enter in the parades. It would contain a beautiful Negro woman riding with the other bathing beauties and stamped with the magical words, Color Added.

1941

HUGH MacLENNAN (b.1907)

The Shadow of Captain Bligh

Not long ago, in the same evening, I listened to my gramophone recording of Haydn's *Mass for St. Cecilia* and then went upstairs and began rereading the account of the mutiny of H.M.S. *Bounty* as written by Nordhoff and Hall. The grand cadences of the Mass kept sounding through my mind, and every now and then I stopped reading to let them swell and subside. I was rereading the book for a purpose and I didn't feel I could put it down. But the counterpoint made me realize with a sensation of shock that Joseph Haydn and Captain Bligh were contemporaries, that the society that had produced and honoured the one was the same society that had employed and respected the other.

Haydn's *Mass for St. Cecilia*, which was partially lost until Dr. Brand recovered it little more than a decade ago, and which hardly anyone had heard performed until it appeared recently in a recording of the Haydn Society, is certainly one of the most sublime works the human spirit has ever created. It seems to me worth all the music composed since the death of Beethoven. Beethoven himself was never able to sustain the power that is manifest here, for his struggle with himself and his medium was too great. Haydn's *Mass*, like the greatest work of Shakespeare, is at once majestic and intimate. Above all it seems effortless, and its joy and triumph are so breathtaking that no one who is moved by music can easily listen to it without reflecting that our modern world has produced no creative genius with his originality, his joyousness or his power.

Yet Haydn was not unique in his time. His career over-lapped those of Bach, Handel, Mozart and Beethoven. Though his age acclaimed him a master, it occurred to nobody in the eighteenth century to think it miraculous that he was able to compose those immensely complex works, some of great length, in so short a time. The best of his contemporaries were equally prolific and worked with equal speed. Handel composed the *Messiah* in a few weeks and Mozart wrote one of his most famous symphonies in a few days. Compared to these eighteenth-century masters, a modern creative artist moves at a snail's pace. Our most famous poets will die leaving behind only a slim body of published verse. The average modern novelist takes from two to three years to write a single good novel. Our musicians – men like Sibelius, Stravinsky and Vaughan Williams – have together, in their long lives, equalled only a fraction of Haydn's output.

How lucky Haydn was to have lived before the radio and the telephone, before civic societies which would have made exorbitant and unavoidable demands on his time and energy, before publicity and interviewers and income tax and traffic horns and metropolitan dailies – to have lived, in short, before the age of distraction.

But *Mutiny on the Bounty* reminded me of the other side of the eighteenth century. The very fact of Captain Bligh implies that the forces which have made ours an age of distraction are far subtler and less avoidable than technical innovations like the telephone and the radio. *Mutiny on the Bounty* should be required reading for anyone who is apt, like myself, to be romantic about past ages and to decry his own. For Captain Bligh was just as typical of the eighteenth century as Haydn was. When I bow before Haydn I must remember that Haydn accepted without question and apparently without remorse the fact that he lived in a world that contained Captain Bligh.

Nothing Mickey Spillane has ever written can be compared in horror to some of the factual scenes in *Mutiny on the*

Bounty. Few passages in literature describe more revolting episodes than those of the *Bounty* sailors being seized in the gangway and flogged until the flesh hung in strips from their backs. With our modern knowledge of neurology, we know that the agonies of these poor creatures did not end when the boatswain's mate ceased swinging the cat. Such beatings damaged the nerve roots along the spine and condemned the victims to permanent suffering. What makes those scenes of torture so unbearable to think about is the added realization that they were not sporadic, were not the offshoots of a psychopathic movement like Naziism, but were standard practice in one of the most stable and reflective societies that ever existed. Captain Bligh's cruelty had the weight and approval of his entire society behind it. When the mutineers were later court-martialled, the court had no interest in determining whether Bligh had been cruel or not. It was interested solely in whether the accused had obeyed to the letter the harsh laws of the British Navy.

Haydn, Bach, Handel and Mozart, sublime spirits full of mercy, with sensibilities exquisitely delicate, knew that men like Bligh were the mainstays of the societies they inhabited. Yet this knowledge which to us would be a shame, felt personally, seldom if ever troubled their dreams or ruffled their serenity. The humanitarianism that disturbed Beethoven a generation later had not dawned when Haydn wrote the *Mass for St. Cecilia.*

Haydn reached his prime in the last moments when it was possible for a creative artist to mind his own business in the sense that his conscience could remain untroubled by the sufferings of the unfortunate. If sailors were flogged to death and peasants had no rights, if a neighbouring country was ruined by famine or pestilence, if laws were unjust or princes cruel, none was Haydn's affair. He was compelled to no empathy in the suffering of others as modern artists are.

It is this awareness of personal responsibility for the welfare of strangers that makes uneasy all men of imagination today, that troubles their work and makes much of it seem tortured, that frustrates it too, for seldom can a modern man of creative imagination do anything concrete to change the world he lives in.

Responsible only to himself, to his family and to his God, Haydn enjoyed a freedom few artists have known since. The result was as glorious as it is inimitable. It is on most of his successors that the shadow of Captain Bligh has fallen and remained.

As Haydn represents the spiritual grandeur of the eighteenth-century imagination, Bligh represents its irresponsibility. In Bligh's own words, it was only through fear and cruelty that the stupid, the weak, the incompetent, the ignorant and the unfortunate could be ruled and compelled to do what their masters considered to be their duty. Unless they were so compelled, the supporters of the system argued, there could be no fineness, no spiritual grandeur, no great literature or beautiful buildings, no masses for St. Cecilia. Civilization, as men of Haydn's day conceived it, could not exist if it yielded to the promptings of a social conscience.

When we realize this it becomes easier to reconcile ourselves to the fact that the world we live in is producing no more Haydns or Mozarts. In the nineteenth century men of imagination turned their attention to the miseries of the world they saw about them, accepted responsibility for it and forever lost the peace and concentration of spirit which enabled the Haydns and Mozarts to devote the full force of their genius to the realization of the gifts God had given them.

Could a modern artist witness a public flogging and then go home and compose exquisite music? Could he even live quietly under a régime that permitted such atrocities and retain his own respect and that of others?

Merely to ask such questions is to answer them. Musicians who took no more active part in the Hitler régime than perform for a Nazi audience have had to spend years as outcasts before western society would accept them again. The social conscience of today demands the service of every artist alive, and does not forgive him if he refuses it.

On the other hand western society did not make outcasts of the physicists, chemists and engineers who served Hitler. Until very recently science reserved for itself the same mental freedom that art enjoyed in Haydn's day. If politicians or monsters used the work of science for evil purposes, the scientists felt no personal responsibility. Enjoying such peace of mind, physicists and chemists have been able to devote the full force of their intellects to their work, and so their work has been more impressive than that of the artists who were their contemporaries. No wonder our age, when it looks for a genius to match Bach or Haydn, does not even stop to search among the ranks of the artists. It picks Einstein.

But when the atomic bomb fell on Hiroshima any number of scientists succumbed to a social conscience as the artists had done long ago. Einstein, Oppenheimer and hundreds of others were overcome with a Hamlet-like self-questioning. If our world lasts long enough it will be interesting to see whether science in the next generation will be as original and productive as it has been in the last three. For a conscience, as Shakespeare knew when he created Hamlet, inhibits action and beclouds genius. Our collective conscience may not have made the modern artist a coward, but it has certainly made him a prisoner.

Consider in contrast to Haydn the life of Albert Schweitzer. Schweitzer began as a musician, and had he lived in the eighteenth century there is no knowing what masterpieces he might have composed. But his conscience would not permit him to devote his entire life to music, so he studied theology and became a minister of the Gospel. Then his conscience told him that preaching was not enough, so he studied medicine and became a doctor. His conscience then informed him that it was self-indulgent to practise medicine in a comfortable European city while there were millions in the world without medical care of any kind. So Schweitzer took his gifts to one of the most primitive parts of Africa. There he has lived and worked ever since, among men so elemental that they can know nothing of Bach or Haydn and cannot even guess at the greatness of the strange healer who came to help them.

Albert Schweitzer will die leaving behind him no tangible or audible monument, no record of objective achievement beyond a few books which are mere by-products of his life and interests. His enormous powers have been spread so widely in the service of others that neither as a musician, nor as a theologian nor as a doctor-scientist, has his work, in itself, been such as to ensure his immortality. An earlier age would have said that Schweitzer had squandered his gifts on savages. But our age, rightly or wrongly, acclaims him as one of its noblest representatives because his life has translated into action, as hardly any other life has done, the highest aspirations of our social conscience.

No other modern artist I know of has made the total sacrifice of his talents that Schweitzer made; yet no modern artist (musician or poet or even the great individualist Picasso) has been undisturbed by the social conscience of our day.

Critics who argue that the subject-matter of modern art is proof of the decadence of modern society don't really understand what they are talking about. Art has always been a reflection of the aspirations and obsessions of its time and the art of today is no exception. If it is haunted and distracted, if it is often ugly and even horrifying, it does not mean that the artists themselves are worse men than Haydn was. It means only that they have not refused, as Haydn did, to accept responsibility for Captain Bligh. For all its horrors, the twentieth century is better than the eighteenth; no politician or dictator who has tried to defy its conscience has been able, in the end, to succeed.

Some time in the future art may reflect the tranquillity that Haydn knew. If it does so, it will not be because those artists of the future are likely to be abler men than artists of today. It will happen because, after this age of transition, the shadow of Captain Bligh has been removed from the whole world.

1954

C. P. SNOW (b.1905)

The Two Cultures

It is about three years since I made a sketch in print of a problem which had been on my mind for some time. It was a problem I could not avoid just because of the circumstances of my life. The only credentials I had to ruminate on the subject at all came through those circumstances, through nothing more than a set of chances. Anyone with similar experience would have seen much the same things and I think made very much the same comments about them. It just happened to be an unusual experience. By training I was a scientist: by vocation I was a writer. That was all. It was a piece of luck, if you like, that arose through coming from a poor home.

But my personal history isn't the point now. All that I need say is that I came to Cambridge and did a bit of research here at a time of major scientific activity. I was privileged to have a ringside view of one of the most wonderful creative periods in all physics. And it happened through the flukes of war – including meeting W. L. Bragg in the buffet on Kettering station on a very cold morning in 1939, which had a determining influence on my practical life – that I was able, and indeed morally forced, to keep that ringside view ever since. So for thirty years I have had to be in touch with scientists not only out of curiosity, but as part of a working existence. During the same thirty years I was trying to shape the books I wanted to write, which in due course took me among writers.

There have been plenty of days when I have spent the

working hours with scientists and then gone off at night with
some literary colleagues. I mean that literally. I have had, of
course, intimate friends among both scientists and writers.
It was through living among these groups and much more, I
think, through moving regularly from one to the other and
back again that I got occupied with the problem of what, long
before I put it on paper, I christened to myself as the 'two
cultures'. For constantly I felt I was moving among two
groups – comparable in intelligence, identical in race, not
grossly different in social origin, earning about the same
incomes – who had almost ceased to communicate at all, who
in intellectual, moral and psychological climate had so little
in common that instead of going from Burlington House or
South Kensington to Chelsea, one might have crossed an
ocean.

In fact, one had travelled much further than across an ocean
– because after a few thousand Atlantic miles, one found
Greenwich Village talking precisely the same language as
Chelsea, and both having about as much communication
with M.I.T. as though the scientists spoke nothing but Tibetan.
For this is not just our problem; owing to some of our educational and social idiosyncrasies, it is slightly exaggerated here,
owing to another English social peculiarity it is slightly mini-
mized; by and large this is a problem of the entire West.

By this I intend something serious. I am not thinking of the
pleasant story of how one of the more convivial Oxford
greats dons – I have heard the story attributed to A. L. Smith
– came over to Cambridge to dine. The date is perhaps the
1890s. I think it must have been at St. John's, or possibly
Trinity. Anyway, Smith was sitting at the right hand of the
President – or Vice-Master – and he was a man who liked to
include all round him in the conversation, although he was
not immediately encouraged by the expressions of his neighbours. He addressed some cheerful Oxonian chit-chat at the
one opposite to him, and got a grunt. He then tried the man on
his own right hand and got another grunt. Then, rather to his
surprise, one looked at the other and said, 'Do you know

what he's talking about?' 'I haven't the least idea.' At this, even Smith was getting out of his depth. But the President, acting as a social emollient, put him at his ease, by saying, 'Oh, those are mathematicians! We never talk to *them*.'

No, I intend something serious. I believe the intellectual life of the whole of western society is increasingly being split into two polar groups. When I say the intellectual life, I mean to include also a large part of our practical life, because I should be the last person to suggest the two can at the deepest level be distinguished. I shall come back to the practical life a little later. Two polar groups: at one pole we have the literary intellectuals, who incidentally while no one was looking took to referring to themselves as 'intellectuals' as though there were no others. I remember G. H. Hardy once remarking to me in mild puzzlement, some time in the 1930s: 'Have you noticed how the word "intellectual" is used nowadays? There seems to be a new definition which certainly doesn't include Rutherford or Eddington or Dirac or Adrian or me. It does seem rather odd, don't y' know.'

Literary intellectuals at one pole – at the other scientists, and as the most representative, the physical scientists. Between the two a gulf of mutual incomprehension – sometimes (particularly among the young) hostility and dislike, but most of all lack of understanding. They have a curious distorted image of each other. Their attitudes are so different that, even on the level of emotion, they can't find much common ground. Non-scientists tend to think of scientists as brash and boastful. They hear Mr. T. S. Eliot, who just for these illustrations we can take as an archetypal figure, saying about his attempts to revive verse-drama, that we can hope for very little, but that he would feel content if he and his co-workers could prepare the ground for a new Kyd or a new Greene. That is the tone, restricted and constrained, with which literary intellectuals are at home: it is the subdued voice of their culture. Then they hear a much louder voice, that of another archetypal figure, Rutherford, trumpeting: 'This is the heroic age of science! This is the Elizabethan age!' Many of us heard that, and a

good many other statements beside which that was mild; and
we weren't left in any doubt whom Rutherford was casting
for the role of Shakespeare. What is hard for the literary intellectuals to understand, imaginatively or intellectually, is that
he was absolutely right.

And compare 'this is the way the world ends, not with a
bang but a whimper' – incidentally, one of the least likely
scientific prophecies ever made – compare that with Rutherford's famous repartee, 'Lucky fellow, Rutherford, always on
the crest of the wave.' 'Well, I made the wave, didn't I?'

The non-scientists have a rooted impression that the scientists are shallowly optimistic, unaware of man's condition. On
the other hand, the scientists believe that the literary intellectuals are totally lacking in foresight, peculiarly unconcerned
with their brother men, in a deep sense anti-intellectual,
anxious to restrict both art and thought to the existential
moment. And so on. Anyone with a mild talent for invective
could produce plenty of this kind of subterranean back-chat.
On each side there is some of it which is not entirely baseless.
It is all destructive. Much of it rests on misinterpretations
which are dangerous. I should like to deal with two of the
most profound of these now, one on each side.

First, about the scientists' optimism. This is an accusation
which has been made so often that it has become a platitude.
It has been made by some of the acutest non-scientific minds
of the day. But it depends upon a confusion between the
individual experience and the social experience, between the
individual condition of man and his social condition. Most of
the scientists I have known well have felt – just as deeply as
the non-scientists I have known well – that the individual
condition of each of us is tragic. Each of us is alone: sometimes we escape from solitariness, through love or affection
or perhaps creative moments, but those triumphs of life are
pools of light we make for ourselves while the edge of the
road is black: each of us dies alone. Some scientists I have
known have had faith in revealed religion. Perhaps with them
the sense of the tragic condition is not so strong. I don't know.

With most people of deep feeling, however high-spirited and happy they are, sometimes most with those who are happiest and most high-spirited, it seems to be right in the fibres, part of the weight of life. That is as true of the scientists I have known best as of anyone at all.

But nearly all of them – and this is where the colour of hope genuinely comes in – would see no reason why, just because the individual condition is tragic, so must the social condition be. Each of us is solitary: each of us dies alone: all right, that's a fate against which we can't struggle – but there is plenty in our condition which is not fate, and against which we are less than human unless we do struggle.

Most of our fellow human beings, for instance, are underfed and die before their time. In the crudest terms, *that* is the social condition. There is a moral trap which comes through the insight into man's loneliness: it tempts one to sit back, complacent in one's unique tragedy, and let the others go without a meal.

As a group, the scientists fall into the trap less than others. They are inclined to be impatient to see if something can be done: and inclined to think that it can be done, until it's proved otherwise. That is their real optimism, and it's an optimism that the rest of us badly need.

In reverse, the same spirit, tough and good and determined to fight it out at the side of their brother men, has made scientists regard the other culture's social attitudes as contemptible. That is too facile: some of them are, but they are a temporary phase and not to be taken as representative.

I remember being cross-examined by a scientist of distinction. 'Why do most writers take on social opinions which would have been thought distinctly uncivilized and *démodé* at the time of the Plantagenets? Wasn't that true of most of the famous twentieth-century writers? Yeats, Pound, Wyndham Lewis, nine out of ten of those who have dominated literary sensibility in our time – weren't they not only politically silly, but politically wicked? Didn't the influence of all they represent bring Auschwitz that much nearer?'

I thought at the time, and I still think, that the correct answer was not to defend the indefensible. It was no use saying that Yeats, according to friends whose judgment I trust, was a man of singular magnanimity of character, as well as a great poet. It was no use denying the facts, which are broadly true. The honest answer was that there is, in fact, a connection, which literary persons were culpably slow to see, between some kinds of early twentieth-century art and the most imbecile expressions of anti-social feeling. That was one reason, among many, why some of us turned our backs on the art and tried to hack out a new or different way for ourselves.

But though many of those writers dominated literary sensibility for a generation, that is no longer so, or at least to nothing like the same extent. Literature changes more slowly than science. It hasn't the same automatic corrective, and so its misguided periods are longer. But it is ill-considered of scientists to judge writers on the evidence of the period 1914–50.

Those are two of the misunderstandings between the two cultures. I should say, since I began to talk about them – the two cultures, that is – I have had some criticism. Most of my scientific acquaintances think that there is something in it, and so do most of the practising artists I know. But I have been argued with by non-scientists of strong down-to-earth interests. Their view is that it is an over-simplification, and that if one is going to talk in these terms there ought to be at least three cultures. They argue that, though they are not scientists themselves, they would share a good deal of the scientific feeling. They would have as little use – perhaps, since they knew more about it, even less use – for the recent literary culture as the scientists themselves. J. H. Plumb, Alan Bullock and some of my American sociological friends have said that they vigorously refuse to be corralled in a cultural box with people they wouldn't be seen dead with, or to be regarded as helping to produce a climate which would not permit of social hope.

I respect those arguments. The number 2 is a very dangerous number: that is why the dialectic is a dangerous process. Attempts to divide anything into two ought to be regarded with much suspicion. I have thought a long time about going in for further refinements: but in the end I have decided against. I was searching for something a little more than a dashing metaphor, a good deal less than a cultural map: and for those purposes the two cultures is about right, and subtilizing any more would bring more disadvantages than it's worth.

At one pole, the scientific culture really is a culture, not only in an intellectual but also in an anthropological sense. That is, its members need not, and of course often do not, always completely understand each other; biologists more often than not will have a pretty hazy idea of contemporary physics; but there are common attitudes, common standards and patterns of behaviour, common approaches and assumptions. This goes surprisingly wide and deep. It cuts across other mental patterns, such as those of religion or politics or class.

Statistically, I suppose slightly more scientists are in religious terms unbelievers, compared with the rest of the intellectual world – though there are plenty who are religious, and that seems to be increasingly so among the young. Statistically also, slightly more scientists are on the Left in open politics – though again, plenty always have called themselves conservatives, and that also seems to be more common among the young. Compared with the rest of the intellectual world. considerably more scientists in this country and probably in the U.S. come from poor families. Yet, over a whole range of thought and behaviour, none of that matters very much. In their working, and in much of their emotional life, their attitudes are closer to other scientists than to non-scientists who in religion or politics or class have the same labels as themselves. If I were to risk a piece of shorthand, I should say that naturally they had the future in their bones.

They may or may not like it, but they have it. That was as true of the conservatives J. J. Thomson and Lindemann as of

the radicals Einstein or Blackett: as true of the Christian
A. H. Compton as of the materialist Bernal: of the aristocrats
Broglie or Russell as of the proletarian Faraday: of those born
rich, like Thomas Merton or Victor Rothschild, as of Rutherford, who was the son of an odd-job handyman. Without
thinking about it, they respond alike. That is what a culture
means.

At the other pole, the spread of attitudes is wider. It is
obvious that between the two, as one moves through intellectual society from the physicists to the literary intellectuals,
there are all kinds of tones of feeling on the way. But I believe
the pole of total incomprehension of science radiates its influence on all the rest. That total incomprehension gives, much
more pervasively than we realize, living in it, an unscientific
flavour to the whole 'traditional' culture, and that unscientific
flavour is often, much more than we admit, on the point of
turning anti-scientific. The feelings of one pole become the
anti-feelings of the other. If the scientists have the future in
their bones, then the traditional culture responds by wishing
the future did not exist. It is the traditional culture, to an
extent remarkably little diminished by the emergence of the
scientific one, which manages the western world.

This polarization is sheer loss to us all. To us as people, and
to our society. It is at the same time practical and intellectual
and creative loss, and I repeat that it is false to imagine that
those three considerations are clearly separable. But for a
moment I want to concentrate on the intellectual loss.

The degree of incomprehension on both sides is the kind of
joke which has gone sour. There are about fifty thousand
working scientists in the country and about eighty thousand
professional engineers or applied scientists. During the war
and in the years since, my colleagues and I have had to inter-
view somewhere between thirty and forty thousand of these –
that is, about twenty-five per cent. The number is large enough
to give us a fair sample, though of the men we talked to most
would still be under forty. We were able to find out a certain
amount of what they read and thought about. I confess that

even I, who am fond of them and respect them, was a bit
shaken. We hadn't quite expected that the links with the
traditional culture should be so tenuous, nothing more than a
formal touch of the cap.

As one would expect, some of the very best scientists had
and have plenty of energy and interest to spare, and we came
across several who had read everything that literary people
talk about. But that's very rare. Most of the rest, when one
tried to probe for what books they had read, would modestly
confess, 'Well, I've *tried* a bit of Dickens', rather as though
Dickens were an extraordinarily esoteric, tangled and dubi-
ously rewarding writer, something like Rainer Maria Rilke.
In fact that is exactly how they do regard him: we thought
that discovery, that Dickens had been transformed into the
type-specimen of literary incomprehensibility, was one of the
oddest results of the whole exercise.

But of course, in reading him, in reading almost any writer
whom we should value, they are just touching their caps to
the traditional culture. They have their own culture, intensive,
rigorous, and constantly in action. This culture contains a
great deal of argument, usually much more rigorous, and
almost always at a higher conceptual level, than literary
persons' arguments – even though the scientists do cheerfully
use words in senses which literary persons don't recognize,
the senses are exact ones, and when they talk about 'subjec-
tive', 'objective', 'philosophy', or 'progressive', they know
what they mean, even though it isn't what one is accustomed
to expect.

Remember, these are very intelligent men. Their culture is
in many ways an exacting and admirable one. It doesn't contain much art, with the exception, an important exception, of
music. Verbal exchange, insistent argument. Long-playing
records. Colour-photography. The ear, to some extent the eye.
Books, very little, though perhaps not many would go so far
as one hero, who perhaps I should admit was further down
the scientific ladder than the people I've been talking about –
who, when asked what books he read, replied firmly and

confidently: 'Books? I prefer to use my books as tools.' It was very hard not to let the mind wander – what sort of tool would a book make? Perhaps a hammer? A primitive digging instrument?

Of books, though, very little. And of the books which to most literary persons are bread and butter, novels, history, poetry, plays, almost nothing at all. It isn't that they're not interested in the psychological or moral or social life. In the social life, they certainly are, more than most of us. In the moral, they are by and large the soundest group of intellectuals we have; there is a moral component right in the grain of science itself, and almost all scientists form their own judgments of the moral life. In the psychological they have as much interest as most of us, though occasionally I fancy they come to it rather late. It isn't that they lack the interests. It is much more that the whole literature of the traditional culture doesn't seem to them relevant to those interests. They are, of course, dead wrong. As a result, their imaginative understanding is less than it could be. They are self-impoverished.

But what about the other side? They are impoverished too – perhaps more seriously, because they are vainer about it. They still like to pretend that the traditional culture is the whole of 'culture', as though the natural order didn't exist. As though the exploration of the natural order was of no interest either in its own value or its consequences. As though the scientific edifice of the physical world was not, in its intellectual depth, complexity and articulation, the most beautiful and wonderful collective work of the mind of man. Yet most non-scientists have no conception of that edifice at all. Even if they want to have it, they can't. It is rather as though, over an immense range of intellectual experience, a whole group was tone-deaf. Except that this tone-deafness doesn't come by nature, but by training, or rather the absence of training.

As with the tone-deaf, they don't know what they miss. They give a pitying chuckle at the news of scientists who have never read a major work of English literature. They dismiss them as ignorant specialists. Yet their own ignorance and their own

specialization is just as startling. A good many times I have
been present at gatherings of people who, by the standards of
the traditional culture, are thought highly educated and who
have with considerable gusto been expressing their incredulity
at the illiteracy of scientists. Once or twice I have been pro-
voked and have asked the company how many of them could
describe the Second Law of Thermodynamics. The response
was cold: it was also negative. Yet I was asking something
which is about the scientific equivalent of: *Have you read a
work of Shakespeare's?*

I now believe that if I had asked an even simpler question –
such as, What do you mean by mass, or acceleration, which is
the scientific equivalent of saying, *Can you read?* – not more
than one in ten of the highly educated would have felt that I
was speaking the same language. So the great edifice of
modern physics goes up, and the majority of the cleverest
people in the western world have about as much insight into it
as their neolithic ancestors would have had.

Just one more of those questions, that my non-scientific
friends regard as being in the worst of taste. Cambridge is a
university where scientists and non-scientists meet every night
at dinner. About two years ago, one of the most astonishing
experiments in the whole history of science was brought off.
I don't mean the sputnik – that was admirable for quite different reasons, as a feat of organization and a triumphant use of
existing knowledge. No, I mean the experiment at Columbia
by Yang and Lee. It is an experiment of the greatest beauty
and originality, but the result is so startling that one forgets
how beautiful the experiment is. It makes us think again
about some of the fundamentals of the physical world. Intui-
tion, common sense – they are neatly stood on their heads.
The result is usually known as the contradiction of parity. If
there were any serious communication between the two cultures, this experiment would have been talked about at every
High Table in Cambridge. Was it? I wasn't here: but I should
like to ask the question.

There seems then to be no place where the cultures meet. I

am not going to waste time saying that this is a pity. It is much worse than that. Soon I shall come to some practical consequences. But at the heart of thought and creation we are letting some of our best chances go by default. The clashing point of two subjects, two disciplines, two cultures – of two galaxies, so far as that goes – ought to produce creative chances. In the history of mental activity that has been where some of the break-throughs came. The chances are there now. But they are there, as it were, in a vacuum, because those in the two cultures can't talk to each other. It is bizarre how very little of twentieth-century science has been assimilated into twentieth-century art. Now and then one used to find poets conscientiously using scientific expressions, and getting them wrong – there was a time when 'refraction' kept cropping up in verse in a mystifying fashion, and when 'polarized light' was used as though writers were under the illusion that it was a specially admirable kind of light.

Of course, that isn't the way that science could be any good to art. It has got to be assimilated along with, and as part and parcel of, the whole of our mental experience, and used as naturally as the rest.

1959

ALDOUS HUXLEY (b.1894)

Tomorrow and Tomorrow and Tomorrow

Between 1800 and 1900 the doctrine of Pie in the Sky gave place, in a majority of Western minds, to the doctrine of Pie on the Earth. The motivating and compensatory Future came to be regarded, not as a state of disembodied happiness, to be enjoyed by me and my friends after death, but as a condition of terrestrial well-being for my children or (if that seemed a bit too optimistic) my grandchildren, or maybe my great-grandchildren. The believers in Pie in the Sky consoled themselves for all their present miseries by the thought of post-humous bliss, and whenever they felt inclined to make other people more miserable than themselves (which was most of the time), they justified their crusades and persecutions by proclaiming, in St. Augustine's delicious phrase, that they were practising a 'benignant asperity', which would ensure the eternal welfare of souls through the destruction or torture of mere bodies in the inferior dimensions of space and time. In our days, the revolutionary believers in Pie on the Earth console themselves for *their* miseries by thinking of the wonderful time people will be having a hundred years from now, and then go on to justify wholesale liquidations and enslavements by pointing to the nobler, humaner world which these atroci-ties will somehow or other call into existence.

Not all the believers in Pie on the Earth are revolution-aries, just as not all believers in Pie in the Sky were persecutors. Those who think mainly of other people's future life tend to become proselytizers, crusaders and heresy hunters. Those who think mainly of their own future life become resigned. The preaching of Wesley and his followers had the effect of reconciling the first generations of industrial workers to their intolerable lot and helped to preserve England from the horrors of a full-blown political revolution.

Today the thought of their great-grandchildren's happiness in the twenty-first century consoles the disillusioned beneficiaries of progress and immunizes them against Communist propaganda. The writers of advertising copy are doing for this generation what the Methodists did for the victims of the first Industrial Revolution.

The literature of the Future and of that equivalent of the Future, the Remote, is enormous. By now the bibliography of Utopia must run into thousands of items. Moralists and political reformers, satirists and science fictioneers – all have contributed their quota to the stock of imaginary worlds. Less picturesque, but more enlightening, than these products of phantasy and idealistic zeal are the forecasts made by sober and well-informed men of science. Three very important prophetic works of this kind have appeared within the last two or three years – *The Challenge of Man's Future* by Harrison Brown, *The Foreseeable Future* by Sir George Thomson, and *The Next Million Years* by Sir Charles Darwin. Sir George and Sir Charles are physicists and Mr. Brown is a distinguished chemist. Still more important, each of the three is something more and better than a specialist.

Let us begin with the longest look into the future – *The Next Million Years*. Paradoxically enough, it is easier, in some ways, to guess what is going to happen in the course of ten thousand centuries than to guess what is going to happen in the course of one century. Why is it that no future tellers are millionaires and that no insurance companies go bankrupt? Their business is the same – foreseeing the future. But whereas the members of one group succeed all the time, the members of the other group succeed, if at all, only occasionally. The reason is simple. Insurance companies deal with statistical averages. Fortune tellers are concerned with particular cases. One can predict with a high degree of precision what is going to happen in regard to very large numbers of things or people. To predict what is going to happen to any particular thing or person is for most of us quite impossible and even for the specially gifted minority exceedingly difficult. The history of the next century involves very large numbers; consequently it is possible to make certain predictions about it with a fairly high degree of certainty. But though we can pretty confidently say that there will be revolutions, battles, massacres, hurricanes, droughts, floods, bumper crops and bad harvests, we cannot specify the dates of these events nor the exact locations, nor their immediate, short-range consequences. But when we take the longer view and consider the much greater numbers involved in the history of the next ten thousand centuries, we find that these ups and downs of human and natural happenings tend to cancel out, so that it becomes possible to plot a curve representing the average of future history, the mean between ages of creativity and ages of decadence, between propitious and unpropitious circumstances, between fluctuating triumph and disaster. This is the actuarial approach to prophecy – sound on the large scale and reliable on the average. It is the kind of approach which permits the prophet to say that there will be dark handsome men in the lives of *x* per cent of women, but not which particular woman will succumb.

A domesticated animal is an animal which has a master who is in a position to teach it tricks and, more importantly, to sterilize it or compel it to breed as he sees fit. Human beings have no masters. Even in his most highly civilized state, Man is a wild species, breeding at random and always propagating his kind to the limit of available food supplies. The amount of available food may be increased by the opening up of new land, by the sudden disappearance, owing to famine, disease or war, of a considerable fraction of the population, or by improvements in agriculture. At any given period of history there is a practical limit to the food supply currently available. Moreover, natural processes and the size of the planet being what they are, there is an absolute limit which can never be passed. Being a wild species, Man will always tend to breed up to the limits of the moment. Consequently very many members of the species must always live on the verge of starvation. This has happened in the past, is happening at the present time, when about sixteen hundred millions of men, women and children are more or less seriously undernourished, and will go on happening for the next million years – by which time we may expect that the species *Homo sapiens* will have turned into some other species, unpredictably unlike ourselves but still, of course, subject to the laws governing the lives of wild animals.

We may not appreciate the fact; but a fact nevertheless it remains: we are living in a Golden Age, the most golden Golden Age of human history – not only of past history, but of future history. For, as Sir Charles Darwin and many others before him have pointed out, we are living like drunken sailors, like the irresponsible heirs of a millionaire uncle. At an ever-accelerating rate we are now squandering the capital of metallic ores and fossil fuels accumulated in the earth's crust during hundreds of millions of years. How long can this spending spree go on? Estimates vary. But all are agreed that within a few centuries, or at most a few millennia, Man will have run through his capital and will be compelled to live, for the remaining nine thousand nine hundred and seventy or eighty centuries of his career as *Homo sapiens,* strictly on income. Sir Charles is of the opinion that Man will successfully make the transition from rich ores to poor ores and even sea water, from coal, oil, uranium and thorium to solar energy and alcohol derived from plants. About as much energy as is now available can be derived from the new sources – but with a far greater expense in man hours, a much larger capital investment in machinery. And the same holds true of the raw materials on which industrial civilization depends. By doing a great deal more work than they are doing now, men will contrive to extract the diluted dregs of the planet's metallic wealth or will fabricate non-metallic substitutes for the elements they have completely used up. In such an event, some human beings will still live fairly well, but not in the style to which we, the squanderers of planetary capital, are accustomed.

Mr. Harrison Brown has his doubts about the ability of the human race to make the transition to new and less concentrated sources of energy and raw materials. As he sees it, there are three possibilities. 'The first and by far the most likely pattern is a return to agrarian existence.' This return, says Mr. Brown, will almost certainly take place unless Man is able not only to make the technological transition to new energy sources and new raw materials, but also to abolish war and at the same time stabilize his population. Sir Charles, incidentally, is convinced that Man will never succeed in stabilizing his population. Birth control may be practised here and there for brief periods. But any nation which limits its population will ultimately be crowded out by nations which have not limited theirs. Moreover, by reducing cut-throat competition within the society which practises it, birth control restricts the action of natural selection. But wherever natural selection is not allowed free play, biological degeneration rapidly sets in. And then there are the short-range, practical difficulties. The rulers of sovereign states have never been able to agree on a common policy in relation to economics, to disarmament, to civil liberties. Is it likely, is it even conceivable, that they will agree on a common policy in relation to the much more ticklish matter of birth control? The answer would seem to be in the negative. And if, by a miracle, they should agree, or if a world government should some day come into existence, how could a policy of birth control be enforced? Answer: only by totalitarian methods and, even so, pretty ineffectively.

Let us return to Mr. Brown and the second of his alternative futures. 'There is a possibility,' he writes, 'that stabilization of population can be achieved, that war can be avoided, and that the resource transition can be successfully negotiated. In that event mankind will be confronted with a pattern which looms on the horizon of events as the second most likely possibility – the completely controlled, collectivized industrial society.' (Such a future society was described in my own fictional essay in Utopianism, *Brave New World*.)

'The third possibility confronting mankind is that of a world-wide free industrial society, in which human beings can live in reasonable harmony with their environment.' This is a cheering prospect; but Mr. Brown quickly chills our optimism by adding that 'it is unlikely that such a pattern can exist for long. It certainly will be difficult to achieve, and it clearly will be difficult to maintain once it is established.'

From these rather dismal speculations about the remoter future it is a relief to turn to Sir George Thomson's prophetic view of what remains of the present Golden Age. So far as easily available power and raw materials are concerned, Western man never had it so good as he has it now and, unless he should choose in the interval to wipe himself out, as he will go on having it for the next three, or five, or perhaps even ten generations. Between the present and the year 2050, when the population of the planet will be at least five billions and perhaps as much as eight billions, atomic power will be added to the power derived from coal, oil and falling water, and Man will dispose of more mechanical slaves than ever before. He will fly at three times the speed of sound, he will travel at seventy knots in submarine liners, he will solve hitherto insoluble problems by means of electronic thinking-machines. High-grade metallic ores will still be plentiful, and research in physics and chemistry will teach men how to use them more effectively and will provide at the same time a host of new synthetic materials. Meanwhile the biologists will not be idle. Various algae, bacteria and fungi will be domesticated, selectively bred and set to work to produce various kinds of food and to perform feats of chemical synthesis which would otherwise be prohibitively expensive. More picturesquely (for Sir George is a man of imagination), new breeds of monkeys will be developed, capable of performing the more troublesome kinds of agricultural work, such as picking fruit, cotton and coffee. Electron beams will be directed on to particular areas of plant and animal chromosomes and, in this way, it may become possible to produce controlled mutations. In the field of medicine, cancer may finally be prevented, while senility ('the whole business of old age is odd and little understood') may be postponed, perhaps almost indefinitely. 'Success,' adds Sir George, 'will come, when it does, from some quite unexpected directions; some discovery in physiology will alter present ideas as to how and why cells grow and divide in the healthy body, and with the right fundamental knowledge, enlightenment will come. It is only the rather easy superficial problems that can be solved by working on them directly; others depend on still undiscovered fundamental knowledge and are hopeless till this has been acquired.'

All in all, the prospects for the industrialized minority of mankind are, in the short run, remarkably bright. Provided we refrain from the suicide of war, we can look forward to very good times indeed. That we shall be discontented with our good time goes without saying. Every gain made by individuals or societies is almost instantly taken for granted. The luminous ceiling towards which we raise our longing eyes becomes, when we have climbed to the next floor, a stretch of disregarded linoleum beneath our feet. But the right to disillusionment is as fundamental as any other in the catalogue. (Actually the right to the pursuit of happiness is nothing else than the right to disillusionment phrased in another way.)

Turning now from the industrialized minority to that vast majority inhabiting the underdeveloped countries, the immediate prospects are much less reassuring. Population in these countries is increasing by more than twenty millions a year, and in Asia at least, according to the best recent estimates, the production of food per head is now ten per cent less than it used to be in 1938. In India the average diet provides about two thousand calories a day – far below the optimum figure. If the country's food production could be raised by forty per cent – and the experts believe that, given much effort and a very large capital investment, it could be increased to this extent within fifteen or twenty years – the available food would provide the present population with twenty-eight hundred calories a day, a figure still below the optimum level. But twenty years from now the population of India will have increased by something like one hundred millions, and the additional food, produced with so much effort and at such great expense, will add little more than a hundred calories to the present woefully inadequate diet. And meanwhile it is not at all probable that a forty per cent increase in food production will in fact be achieved within the next twenty years.

The task of industrializing the underdeveloped countries, and of making them capable of producing enough food for their peoples, is difficult in the extreme. The industrialization of the West was made possible by a series of historical accidents. The inventions which launched the Industrial Revolution were made at precisely the right moment. Huge areas of empty land in America and Australasia were being opened up by European colonists or their descendants. A great surplus of cheap food became available, and it was upon this surplus that the peasants and farm labourers, who migrated to the towns and became factory hands, were enabled to live and multiply their kind. Today there are no empty lands – at any rate none that lend themselves to easy cultivation – and the over-all surplus of food is small in relation to present populations. If a million Asiatic peasants are taken off the land and set to work in factories, who will produce the food which their labour once provided? The obvious answer is: machines. But how can the million new factory workers make the necessary machines if, in the meanwhile, they are not fed? Until they make the machines, they cannot be fed from the land they once cultivated; and there are no surpluses of cheap food from other, emptier countries to support them in the interval.

And then there is the question of capital. 'Science,' you often hear it said, 'will solve all our problems.' Perhaps it will, perhaps it won't. But before science can start solving any practical problems, it must be applied in the form of usable technology. But to apply science on any large scale is extremely expensive. An underdeveloped country cannot be industrialized, or given an efficient agriculture, except by the investment of a very large amount of capital. But what is capital? It is what is left over when the primary needs of a society have been satisfied. In most of Asia the primary needs of most of the population are never satisfied; consequently almost nothing is left over. Indians can save about one-hundredth of their per capita income. Americans can save between one-tenth and one-sixth of what they make. Since the income of Americans is much higher than that of Indians, the amount of available capital in the United States is about seventy times as great as the amount of available capital in India. To those who have shall be given and from those who have not shall be taken away even that which they have. If the underdeveloped countries are to be industrialized, even partially, and made self-supporting in the matter of food, it will be necessary to establish a vast international Marshall Plan providing subsidies in grain, money, machinery, and trained manpower. But all these will be of no avail, if the population in the various underdeveloped areas is permitted to increase at anything like the present rate. Unless the population of Asia can be stabilized, all attempts at industrialization will be doomed to failure and the last state of all concerned will be far worse than the first – for there will be many more people for famine and pestilence to destroy, together with much more political discontent, bloodier revolutions and more abominable tyrannies.

1956

Notes

Jonathan Swift's *A Modest Proposal* was published in Dublin in 1729. It appears here in a modernized version prepared by Swift's best editor, Professor Herbert Davis of Oxford.

The chapter by John Stuart Mill is the first of the five chapters which comprise *On Liberty*, published in London in 1859.

Our selection from G. K. Chesterton is the first two-thirds of the chapter entitled 'The Flag of the World' from *Orthodoxy*, published in London in 1908.

E. M. Forster's 'What I Believe' was written in 1939 and later collected by the author in *Two Cheers for Democracy*, published in London in 1951.

Stephen Leacock's 'Oxford As I See It' was originally a lecture prepared for use in a speaking tour of the British Isles. It was first printed in *My Discovery of England*, published in London in 1922.

Max Beerbohm's 'The Crime' was first published in London in 1920 and collected in the same year into the author's *And Even Now*.

Virginia Woolf's 'How Should One Read a Book?' first appeared in the form given here in Mrs. Woolf's *The Common Reader, Second Series*, published in London in 1932.

'Politics and the English Language' was first printed in 1946 and later collected by George Orwell in the volume *Shooting an Elephant and Other Essays*, published in London in 1950.

'In Praise of Idleness', written by Bertrand Russell in 1932, later became the lead essay in the author's *In Praise of Idleness and Other Essays*, published in London in 1935.

Herbert Read's *To Hell with Culture*, which carries the sub-title 'Democratic Values Are New Values', was published in London in 1941. Our selection from the book comprises the two sections entitled 'The Strayed Riveter' and 'Pots and Pans'.

'On a Florida Key' first appeared in New York in 1941 and was collected the following year into E. B. White's *One Man's Meat*. Our selection comprises the first two-thirds of the original essay.

'The Shadow of Captain Bligh' was collected by Hugh MacLennan into the volume *Thirty and Three*, published in Toronto in 1954.

The 1959 Rede Lecture at Cambridge University was given by C. P. Snow under the title *The Two Cultures and the Scientific Revolution*. Our selection comprises approximately the first third of the lecture.

'Tomorrow and Tomorrow and Tomorrow' was first collected by Aldous Huxley into the volume *Adonis and the Alphabet and Other Essays*, published in London in 1956.

R. C.
C. K.